Praise for
THE JEWISH TRIVIA AND INFORMATION BOOK™
Trivia Judaica

"This is a remarkable book. It is amazing how much non-trivial information the author included in these impressive, enlightening pages."

—**Dr. Philip Birnbaum**, author and translator,
Jewish liturgical literature
The Daily Prayer Book,
The High Holyday Machzor
The Abridged Mishneh Torah

"A delightful book filled with not-so-trivial information"

—**Blu Greenberg**, President JWB Jewish Book Council,
author of *How to Run a Traditional Jewish Household*

"Ian Shapolsky's JEWISH TRIVIA AND INFORMATION BOOK offers both education and recreation. It is a book not only to read but to play—a treasure between covers."

—**M. Hirsch Goldberg**, author of
The Jewish Connection
Just Because They're Jewish

"THE JEWISH TRIVIA AND INFORMATION BOOK is an easy and enjoyable way to become well informed about every aspect of Jewish life."

—**Rabbi Alfred J. Kolatch**, author of
The Jewish Book of Why
The Second Jewish Book of Why

**On the *B'nai B'rith Jewish Monthly* bestseller list for over ten months.

**The bestselling Jewish paperback in America.

**Over 100,000 copies in print.

"This is a remarkable book."—**Dr. Philip Birnbaum,**
author and translator: *The Daily Prayer Book,*
The High Holyday Machzor, The Abridged Mishnah Torah.

THE NEW VERSION OF THE #**1** JEWISH BESTSELLER

The Second Jewish Trivia & Information Book™

Trivia Judaica™ II

BY IAN SHAPOLSKY

Featuring Jewish questions to entertain, educate, amuse,
challenge and stimulate on:

✡ Arts and Culture ✡ Personalities and Current Events
✡ History and Religion ✡ Geography and Language
✡ . . . and the world of Jewish women

A Shapolsky Book
Published by Shapolsky Books
a division of
Steimatzky Publishing of North America, Inc.

Typography by Type Network (KTN)
Cover design by Mike Stromberg

10 9 8 7 6 5 4 3 2 1

1st Edition January 1986

Library of Congress Cataloging in Publication Data
Shapolsky, Ian

The Second Jewish Trivia and Information Book.
TRIVIA JUDAICA II
1. Jews—History. I. Title.

ISBN 0-933503-45-8

DEDICATION

For my parents, Anita and Meyer,
whose help was appreciated.

For my sister Lisa, and her family.

For my grandparents and their
family.

—I.S.

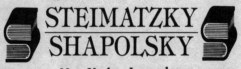

STEIMATZKY/SHAPOLSKY

New York   Jerusalem
Tel Aviv

ACKNOWLEDGEMENTS

I would like to sincerely thank the various librarians in the Judaica departments of the New York City libraries I visited in the course of completing this project. They graciously offered countless hours of their time and guided me to the research materials crucial to the success of this endeavor.

I also wish to express my gratitude to the most important person involved in the work of this book: its editor, Eve Gittelson, to whom I owe inestimable thanks. She provided indispensable advice, criticism and suggestions—including the magnificent idea of creating a new category about the world of Jewish women. Her dedication has made this a stronger and more well rounded final volume.

I was especially fortunate that Natalie Gittelson, so generously reviewed parts of this work offering numerous insightful comments. I am indebted for the valuable contributions she made.

I also want to express my thanks to Michael Freiser for reviewing parts of the manuscript and for his knowledge and discerning comments.

To the assistant editors, Bruce Whyte, Bella Kogan and Judy Friedman—my gratitude for their help.

In the event that any errors or misinterpretations occur in these pages, I alone bear full responsibility.

Finally THE SECOND JEWISH TRIVIA AND INFORMATION BOOK owes its greatest debt to you the readers who purchased the first JEWISH TRIVIA BOOK. Your support inspired me to do the hard but fulfilling work of searching out and compiling the thousands of new questions that were the source material for this edition.

Ian Shapolsky
October, 1985
New York City

**Special thanks for new questions and
suggested corrections from our readers.**

I am indebted to the many kind readers and eminent Jewish scholars who sent me ideas for this book and who assisted in identifying existing questions-and-answers in the first edition that may have needed further clarification. Hopefully this printing will be totally free of errors. But if not, I await and encourage your letters pointing out corrections.

Thank you: Harold Akrongold, East Rockaway, NY
Leslie R. Axelrod, New York, NY
David Fisher, Jupiter, FL
Rabbi Nathan Goldberg, Brooklyn, NY
Joe Hartman, South Farmingdale, NY
Rena G. Kunis, Bellerose, NY
I. B. Lyon, Hagerstown, MD
Rafael Medoff, Jerusalem, Israel
Isaac E. Mozeson, New York, NY
Sherry Nagar, Selden, New York
Aaron S. Polinsky, New York, NY
Gerald A. Schwartz, Hartsdale, NY
Susan Silverman, Brooklyn, NY
Ken Witt, East Brunswick, NJ

file: ack-2-3

INTRODUCTION

Readers often ask why I call this THE JEWISH TRIVIA AND IN-FORMATION BOOK since there is nothing trivial about Judaism or Jewish history. Mostly for the fun of it; and in the hope of focusing attention on this rich and extraordinary culture and heritage.

On a more personal level, to compile, research, and write THE SECOND JEWISH TRIVIA AND INFORMATION BOOK has been an exciting, rewarding, informative and stimulating experience. In order to locate the most diverse and entertaining questions, I pored through hundreds of books, encyclopedias, biographies, newspapers, magazines and journals. Fortunately, Jewish culture and history brims over with such extraordinary people and events that I did not have to search far to find thousands of exceptional questions. The problem became which to use here and which to save for Volume Three.

Because of the convenient structure of the questions and answers, this book is especially well suited for use as a quiz or a game among groups of people who consider themselves to be knowledgeable about Jewish topics. Challenge your friends and family and discover who is best informed on subjects of Jewish interest.

If you, the reader, wish to offer any comments, suggestions or new questions, I would warmly welcome them. If your questions are accepted for the next edition we will send you Volume Three as a gift. Please address all responses to:

The Jewish Trivia Contest
Steimatzky Publishing
56 East 11th Street
New York, New York 10003

CURRENT
EVENTS

1. ► President Reagan's historic mistake in going to the German military cemetery at Bitburg where Nazi officers are buried was compounded by this ill-conceived comparison . . . ?

WOMEN

2. ► Name three Arab countries in which women are denied the right to vote?

ARTS &
CULTURE

3. ► Which prolific Jewish author has the longest entry in *Who's Who in America* because of the numerous books he has written?

PEOPLE

4. ► During the years prior to the Holocaust, this Zionist leader prophetically warned Europe's Jews to "Liquidate the exile before the exile liquidates you . . ."?

RELIGION

5. ► Why are autopsies not permitted under Jewish law?

HISTORY

6. ► This trial began in Jerusalem on April 11, 1961 and ended on May 31, 1962, when the accused was found guilty and hanged . . . ?

LANGUAGE

7. ► In Germany, what word was inscribed on the yellow stars that the Nazis forced all Jews to wear . . . ?

GEOGRAPHY

8. ► Ben-Gurion was offered this location, in 1946, for a Jewish homeland . . . ?

ANSWERS

1. ► He equated the murderers and their victims, claiming that both had suffered equally.

2. ► There are seven in all: Saudi Arabia, Kuwait, Libya, Jordan, Oman, Qatar, United Arab Emirates.

3. ► Isaac Asimov.

4. ► Vladimir (Ze'ev) Jabotinsky.

5. ► Jews take the position that man was created in the image of God. The holiness of human beings demand that we do not tamper with them.

6. ► The trial of Adolf Eichmann. He organized the Nazi extermination program while directing Sub-Department IV 4b of the Reich Security Division.

7. ► Jude. (Jew in German.)

8. ► An area in Vietnam was offered by Ho Chi Minh.

CURRENT EVENTS

9. ► The disputed remains of this long-sought Nazi were found in Embo, Brazil in 1985 . . . ?

WOMEN

10. ► In 1972, Sally J. Preisand became the first Jewish woman to . . . ?

ARTS & CULTURE

11. ► This noted film about modern Israel's early history was based on the story of a U.S. Army Colonel who joined the Israeli Army . . . ?

PEOPLE

12. ► Which African dictator declared his admiration for Hitler's "Final Solution"?

RELIGION

13. ► The story of Purim begins with a conflict between King Ahashverosh and Queen Vashti. Biblical commentators disagree on Vashti's fate. What are the two main opinions?

HISTORY

14. ► In the last Presidential election, the Mondale/Ferraro ticket received approximately this percentage of the Jewish vote (within 10% accuracy) . . . ?

LANGUAGE

15. ► *Aliyah* refers to a Jew who migrates to Israel. It means literally . . . ?

GEOGRAPHY

16. ► This deep sea port is Israel's outlet to Africa and Asia; its subtropical waters make it a major Israeli resort . . . ?

 (Answers next page.)

ANSWERS

CURRENT EVENTS	9. ▶ Dr. Joseph Mengele (also known as Auschwitz's Angel of Death).
WOMEN	10. ▶ Be ordained a rabbi (in the American Reform Movement).
ARTS & CULTURE	11. ▶ "Cast a Giant Shadow"—The Story of Colonel David "Mickey" Marcus.
PEOPLE	12. ▶ Idi Amin of Uganda.
RELIGION	13. ▶ She was either executed or banished from the kingdom.
HISTORY	14. ▶ 70% (according to exit polls conducted by two TV networks).
LANGUAGE	15. ▶ To ascend.
GEOGRAPHY	16. ▶ Eilat.

CURRENT
EVENTS

17. ► Political and military experts speculate that Israel has at least 100 of these dangerous weapons. . . ?

WOMEN

18. ► This American Jewish movie actress, who dated Henry Kissinger, was born Jill Oppenheim. . . ?

ARTS &
CULTURE

19. ► Which Academy-Award winning screenwriter created advertisements criticizing the Allies for refusing to rescue Jews from Hitler?

PEOPLE

20. ► In 1985, the Congressional Gold Medal of Achievement was presented to this survivor of the Holocaust. . . ?

RELIGION

21. ► The walls of Jericho collapsed after this kind of horn was blown how many times. . . ?

HISTORY

22. ► This Israeli war followed a period of deceptive calm, during which the Arab states reorganized and rebuilt their military power. . . ?

LANGUAGE

23. ► What does the Moslem word *Jihad* mean?

GEOGRAPHY

24. ► Before 1967, how wide was Israel at its narrowest point?

ANSWERS

CURRENT EVENTS

25. ► This anti-Semitic incident occurred during the 1985 Shiite terrorist hijacking of TWA Flight 847...?

WOMEN

26. ► She is the Jewish author of *Looking For Mr. Goodbar* and *August*...?

ARTS & CULTURE

27. ► What is the stage name of the Jewish, Hungarian-born, actor Lazlo Lowenstein, famous for his sinister characters?

PEOPLE

28. ► What Vice-President of the United States kept a Torah in his Senate chamber office?

RELIGION

29. ► Which two Biblical animals could talk, and to whom did they talk?

HISTORY

30. ► The Balfour Declaration was written in the form of a letter to which prominent, Jewish British philanthropist?

LANGUAGE

31. ► A General in the Israel Defense Forces is known in Hebrew as ...?

GEOGRAPHY

32. ► The Tower of Babel was supposed to reach this location...?

(Answers next page.)

ANSWERS

CURRENT
EVENTS

CURRENT
EVENTS

25. ► Passengers with Jewish-sounding names were separated by the terrorists from the other passengers.

WOMEN

26. ► Judith Rossner.

ARTS &
CULTURE

27. ► Peter Lorre.

PEOPLE

28. ► Vice-President Hubert Humphrey. (It resided in a gift case in his office.)

RELIGION

29. ► A snake spoke to Eve; an ass to Balaam.

HISTORY

30. ► Lord Rothschild.

LANGUAGE

31. ► "Aluf."

GEOGRAPHY

32. ► Heaven.

CURRENT
EVENTS

33. ► Colonel Muammar Qadaffi has a "pirate ship" sailing off the coasts of Morocco and Tunisia engaged in this outrageous anti-Semitic activity . . . ?

WOMEN

34. ► This granddaughter of a *shochet* (ritual slaughterer), a Ph.D. in electrical engineering and design engineer for RCA, was the first Jewish-American astronaut . . . ?

ARTS &
CULTURE

35. ► This versatile Jewish author played the role of architect Stanford White in the movie *Ragtime* . . . ?

PEOPLE

36. ► He was the U.S. Labor Secretary, the U.S. Ambassador to the U.N., and a U.S. Supreme Court Justice—all within 5 years . . . ?

RELIGION

37. ► This holiday involves the tradition of sending gifts of food . . . ?

HISTORY

38. ► Who built the First Temple and royal palace in Jerusalem and made Israel a great nation of traders?

LANGUAGE

39. ► What is the woman's section in an Orthodox synagogue called in Hebrew?

GEOGRAPHY

40. ► The Dead Sea scrolls were found in a cave in this city near the Dead Sea . . . ?

      (Answers next page.)

ANSWERS

33. ► Broadcasting appeals to the Moroccan
and Tunisian people to kill local Jews.

34. ► Judith A. Resnick.

35. ► Norman Mailer.

36. ► Arthur Goldberg.

37. ► Purim. (The presents are called
"Shalach Manot").

38. ► King Solomon (David's son, 961 BCE
to 920 BCE).

39. ► "Ezrat Nashim."

40. ► Qumran.

CURRENT
EVENTS

41. ▶ *Amal*, the main Lebanese Shiite Moslem militia, is led by this ostensible "moderate"...?

WOMEN

42. ▶ In 1963, what Jewish feminist wrote the classic text of the women's movement, and what was the title of her book?

ARTS &
CULTURE

43. ▶ Jewish artists Jerry Siegel and Joe Shuster created this world-famous comic book character in the 1930's...?

PEOPLE

44. ▶ The men's bathroom in Jerusalem's Israel Museum is affectionately named after this famous Israeli politician...?

RELIGION

45. ▶ How many days did Jonah spend in the belly of the whale?

HISTORY

46. ▶ On December 11, 1917, this British General led the forces that entered Jerusalem and ended four centuries of Ottoman rule over the Holy Land...?

LANGUAGE

47. ▶ Ladino (the Sephardic Jewish language) is a derivation of what two languages?

GEOGRAPHY

48. ▶ Israeli super-spy Eli Cohen operated primarily in this country?

ANSWERS

	41. ►	Nabih Berri.
	42. ►	Betty Friedan, "The Feminine Mystique."
	43. ►	Superman.
	44. ►	Jerusalem's mayor, Teddy Kollek.
	45. ►	Three days.
	46. ►	General Allenby (formally known as Viscount Edmund Henry Hyman Allenby).
	47. ►	Spanish and Turkish. (It is often mistakenly assumed that Ladinos' origin is Hebrew).
	48. ►	Syria. (He rose to the level of second in command of the Syrian government.)

CURRENT
EVENTS

49. ► This recently formed right-leaning Israeli political party won five seats in the Knesset and became Israel's third largest party?

WOMEN

50. ► What was the name of Moses' mother?

ARTS &
CULTURE

51. ► This Jewish speechwriter for Vice-President Spiro Agnew, now a syndicated columnist, coined the phrase "nattering nabobs of negativism"...?

PEOPLE

52. ► This US Senator, who gained prominence during the Watergate hearings, publically considered converting to Judaism...?

RELIGION

53. ► The destruction of the Temple resulted in these two crises...?

HISTORY

54. ► On the night of November 9th, 1938, the Nazis burned 191 synagogues, destroyed 815 Jewish shops, and smashed the windows of Jewish homes and stores throughout Germany. That evening came to be known as...?

LANGUAGE

55. ► What is *chametz*?

GEOGRAPHY

56. ► When did large numbers of Jews begin to settle in Eastern Europe?

ANSWERS

CURRENT EVENTS
49. ► The nationalist Tehiya Party (led by Geula Cohen and General Rafael "Raful" Eitan).

WOMEN
50. ► Yocheved.

ARTS & CULTURE
51. ► William Safire.

PEOPLE
52. ► Senator Daniel Inouye of Hawaii.

RELIGION
53. ► The Jewish people lost their land and they believed the Divine Presence—the "shekhina"—had departed from Jerusalem.

HISTORY
54. ► "Kristallnacht," or the night of broken glass.

LANGUAGE
55. ► Leavened bread, that is not to be seen, eaten, enjoyed or profited from during Pesach.

GEOGRAPHY
56. ► In the 13th century. (Polish kings wanted business-oriented Jews to help diversify Poland's agricultural economy into a commerce-oriented one.)

CURRENT
EVENTS
57. ► How many Jews are there in Libya?

WOMEN
58. ► In 1972, a 13-year-old Soviet Jewish girl, Marina Tiempkin, was given permission to emigrate to Israel with her father, but she never made it. What happened to her?

ARTS &
CULTURE
59. ► What Jewish comedian and specialist in crude humor said, "If it weren't for pickpockets, I'd have no sex life at all"?

PEOPLE
60. ► What do Bobby Fisher, Karl Marx, Heinrich Heine and Benjamin Disraeli have in common?

RELIGION
61. ► This Jewish-born leader is the Father of Christianity . . . ?

HISTORY
62. ► In 1863, the most anti-Semitic act in American history occurred when this U.S. General and eventual Republican Presidential candidate ordered all Jews expelled from Tennessee . . . ?

LANGUAGE
63. ► The last three words of the Passover Seder *Le-shanah Ha-ba-ah B'Yerusha-layim* mean . . . ?

GEOGRAPHY
64. ► During the Jewish exodus from Egypt what two bodies of water parted?

ANSWERS

CURRENT EVENTS   **57. ▶ None. The last remaining Libyan Jews were driven out after savage pogroms in 1967.**

WOMEN   **58. ▶ She was kidnapped by the KGB and has not been heard from since.**

ARTS & CULTURE   **59. ▶ Rodney Dangerfield.**

PEOPLE   **60. ▶ They were all Jews who converted to Christianity.**

RELIGION   **61. ▶ Jesus Christ.**

HISTORY   **62. ▶ General Ulysses S. Grant (in his infamous General Order #11. President Lincoln immediately revoked this order when it was brought to his attention).**

LANGUAGE   **63. ▶ Next year in Jerusalem.**

GEOGRAPHY   **64. ▶ The Red Sea and the Jordan River.**

CURRENT
EVENTS

65. ▶ This Israeli leader was directly involved with the following political contro-
versies: building a stadium near Sanhe-
dria Marhevet, fighting against the Ra-
mat Road demonstrators and destroy-
ing the illegally built synagogue in Gilo
. . . ?

WOMEN

66. ▶ This Jewish heroine parachuted into
Hungary during the Holocaust in order
to rescue Jews, but was captured and
tortured to death by the Nazis . . . ?

ARTS &
CULTURE

67. ▶ He is the non-Jewish conductor of the
Israeli Philharmonic . . . ?

PEOPLE

68. ▶ These two well-known Canadian
Jewish entrepreneurs own the Montreal
Canadians ice hockey team and Sea-
gram's whiskey and beverage company
. . . ?

RELIGION

69. ▶ Synagogues throughout time have had
these three major functions . . . ?

HISTORY

70. ▶ This famous 1916 agreement provided
for joint Anglo-French-Russian control
of all parts of Palestine containing holy
places . . . ?

LANGUAGE

71. ▶ This Hebrew name for God appears on
mezuzahs . . . ?

GEOGRAPHY

72. ▶ The Jews of Spain as well as this less
publicized country were faced with the
decision of death or expulsion if they
did not convert to Christianity . . . ?

ANSWERS

CURRENT EVENTS   65. ► Mayor Teddy Kollek of Jerusalem.

WOMEN   66. ► Hannah Senesh.

ARTS & CULTURE   67. ► Zubin Mehta.

PEOPLE   68. ► Edgar and Peter Bronfman.

RELIGION   69. ► A house of assembly (Beth Ha Keneseth), a house of study (Beth Ha Midrash), and a house of prayer (Beth Ha Tefillah).

HISTORY   70. ► The Tripartite (Sykes-Picot) Agreement of 1916.

LANGUAGE   71. ► "Shaddai."

GEOGRAPHY   72. ► Portugal.

CURRENT
EVENTS

73. ► These new Israelis protested against the Chief Rabbinate's ruling that they undergo "conversion" to Judaism by means of immersion in a *mikvah*, the Jewish ritual bath . . . ?

WOMEN

74. ► This noted Biblical woman, the subject of a Book of the Bible, was a convert to Judaism . . . ?

ARTS &
CULTURE

75. ► This Jewish movie maker directed the motion picture *Exodus* . . . ?

PEOPLE

76. ► He was prime minister of Israel during the 1956 Sinai Campaign . . . ?

RELIGION

77. ► The explanation for Jews being "chosen people" is based on this principle . . . ?

HISTORY

78. ► Only this superpower showed sympathy for the Zionist movement before World War I, giving serious consideration to Theodor Herzl's 1902 plea that Jewish development of the Sinai Peninsula be facilitated . . . ?

LANGUAGE

79. ► What is *Gematria*?

GEOGRAPHY

80. ► This country's National Bank admitted in a recent study, that it had helped to finance the Nazi war-machine during World War II by accepting gold stolen by the Nazis from Jews and the treasuries of occupied countries . . . ?

ANSWERS

73. ► The recent emigrants to Israel, the Ethiopian Jews. (The rabbis could not agree on the Jewish status of the Ethiopian Jews.)

WOMEN 74. ► Ruth.

ARTS &
CULTURE 75. ► Otto Preminger.

PEOPLE 76. ► David Ben-Gurion.

RELIGION 77. ► That they had an ethical role to play through the practice of their religion.

HISTORY 78. ► Great Britain.

LANGUAGE 79. ► A mystical method of explaining Hebrew words according to the numerical value of the individual letters. (Known today as numerology.)

GEOGRAPHY 80. ► The Swiss National Bank. (The study was written by a former archivist of the Swiss banking system.)

CURRENT
EVENTS

81. ► What is unique about the amount of U.S. aid given to Israel in the fiscal year 1985?

WOMEN

82. ► This American Jewish author wrote *Generation Without Memory* the story of her personal Jewish awakening. . . ?

ARTS &
CULTURE

83. ► Which famous American restaurant chain serves kosher ice cream. . . ?

PEOPLE

84. ► Which leader of the Jewish under-ground in pre-state Israel assumed the name "Rabbi Israel Sassover," when he hid from the British. . . ?

RELIGION

85. ► This seminary trains American Reform rabbis and was founded in Cincinnati by Isaac Mayer Wise. . . ?

HISTORY

86. ► What was embarrassing to the U.S. government about the post World War II activities of Nazi war criminal Klaus Barbie. . . ?

LANGUAGE

87. ► The Yiddish term *tummel* translates to . . . ?

GEOGRAPHY

88. ► A reconstucted model of The Holy Temple—built by King Herod—is found in this Jerusalem hotel. . . ?

(Answers next page.)

ANSWERS

81. ► All U.S. aid has been in the form of grants not requiring repayment. (Much of the aid remains in the U.S. to pay American manufacturers for necessary weapons systems.)

82. ► Ann Roiphe.

83. ► Howard Johnson's.

84. ► Menachem Begin.

85. ► Hebrew Union College.

86. ► He was employed by the American government from 1947 to 1950 in the U.S. Counter Intelligence Corps. (It has also been alleged that U.S. officials gave him false identity papers so he could avoid earlier arrest attempts.)

87. ► A commotion.

88. ► The Holyland Hotel.

22

CURRENT
EVENTS

89. ► What did the C.I.A., the State Department and the U.S. Air Force recently join together to do that was of significance to the entire Jewish world?

WOMEN

90. ► This former Jewish wife of Cary Grant was born Samile Diane Friessen...?

ARTS &
CULTURE

91. ► This best-selling gentile author recently wrote a book on Jewish Americans entitled *The Rest of Us*...?

PEOPLE

92. ► Born Lev Davidovich Bronstein, this Bolshevik revolutionary played a key role in the Communists' seizure of power in Russia. In 1940, he was murdered by his rivals in the Soviet hierarchy...?

RELIGION

93. ► Philadelphia's Liberty Bell monument has the following inscription: "Proclaim liberty throughout all the land unto all the inhabitants thereof." It is a quote from this book of the Old Testament...?

HISTORY

94. ► On this date, Israel was admitted as a member to the United Nations...?

LANGUAGE

95. ► *Fedayeen* is the Arab word which means...?

GEOGRAPHY

96. ► The hijacking of TWA Flight 847 occurred at this international airport...?

ANSWERS

89. ► **They coordinated the successful Ethiopian Jewish rescue mission.**

WOMEN
90. ► **Dyan Cannon.**

ARTS &
CULTURE
91. ► **Stephen Birmingham (who also wrote "Our Crowd").**

PEOPLE
92. ► **Leon Trotsky.**

RELIGION
93. ► **Leviticus.**

HISTORY
94. ► **May 11, 1949. (Statehood was achieved on May 14, 1948, but it took an additional year to formalize entry into the United Nations.)**

LANGUAGE
95. ► **"Men of sacrifice."**

GEOGRAPHY
96. ► **Athens International Airport.**

24

CURRENT
EVENTS

97. ► The year 1985 marked the 12th gathering of world Jewish sportsmen. This event is held in Israel every four years and is known as...?

WOMEN

98. ► This Jewish movie actress played leading roles in *Terms of Endearment, An Officer and a Gentleman* and *Urban Cowboy*...?

ARTS &
CULTURE

99. ► This Pulitzer Prize-winning Jewish photographer took the famous photo of six marines raising the American flag at Iwo Jima...?

PEOPLE

100. ► These five Jewish lawyers served on the U.S. Supreme Court...?

RELIGION

101. ► Born in Paris to Polish Jewish immigrants, Aaron Lustiger is renowned for having risen to which high position within the Roman Catholic Church ...?

HISTORY

102. ► Spanish Jew Luis De Torres acted as an interpreter for this noted explorer...?

LANGUAGE

103. ► What Hebrew song is sung on Friday night, at the onset of the Sabbath...?

GEOGRAPHY

104. ► The Jews of India, living primarily in Bombay and Cochin, call themselves by this name ...?

ANSWERS

97. ► The "Maccabiah" Games.

98. ► Debra Winger.

99. ► Joe Rosenthal.

100. ► Benjamin Cardozo, Louis Brandeis, Arthur Goldberg, Abraham Fortas, and Felix Frankfurter.

101. ► The Catholic Archbishop of Paris. (His new name is Jean Marie Cardinal Lustiger. He was protected by gentiles during the war and assumed a Christian identity to survive.)

102. ► Christopher Columbus. (Torres was a Marrano, expelled from Spain in 1492—the same year Columbus set sail.)

103. ► "Lecha Dodi."

104. ► Bene Israel (House of Israel).

CURRENT
EVENTS

105. ▶ This recently deported Nazi is due to stand trial in Lyon, France in late 1985...?

WOMEN

106. ▶ These two Jewish comediennes became known for their roles in the series *Saturday Night Live*...?

ARTS &
CULTURE

107. ▶ The Jewish actor famous for his cowboy roles, had a number-one hit record called *Ringo*, in 1964...?

PEOPLE

108. ▶ This famous Zionist leader suggested the establishment of a Jewish homeland in Uganda...?

RELIGION

109. ▶ Who was the very first Jewish sailor, referred to repeatedly in the Bible?

HISTORY

110. ▶ Located in New York City, this world-renowned institution was the first Jewish hospital in the United States ...?

LANGUAGE

111. ▶ What is the traditional Yiddish Shabbos greeting?

GEOGRAPHY

112. ▶ This nation has the largest Jewish population in South America...?

ANSWERS

CURRENT
EVENTS
113. ► 5000 Israelis have been waiting nine or more years for this basic public utility service . . . ?

WOMEN
114. ► This female convert to Judaism said, "Your people shall be my people, and your God my God" . . . ?

ARTS &
CULTURE
115. ► Professor Gershom Sholem wrote the definitive biography of this seventeenth Century False Messiah . . . ?

PEOPLE
116. ► In 1905 this chemist became the first Jew ever to win a Nobel Prize . . . ?

RELIGION
117. ► Perhaps the most renowned Jewish philosopher of all time, this sage was also a famous medical educator who served as personal physician to the Sultan of Egypt . . . ?

HISTORY
118. ► This Ireland-born President of Israel attended Cambridge University and began his career in politics as an announcer on the BBC . . . ?

LANGUAGE
119. ► What is *lashon hara*?

GEOGRAPHY
120. ► This partially excavated archeological park just outside the walls of Jerusalem's Old City, was opened to the public in the summer of 1985 . . . ?

       (Answers next page.)

ANSWERS

CURRENT EVENTS	113. ▶	**Telephone installation. Israel has a severe shortage of phone equipment.**
WOMEN	114. ▶	**Ruth (the Moabite).**
ARTS & CULTURE	115. ▶	**Shabatai Zvi.**
PEOPLE	116. ▶	**Adolph Von Bayer.**
RELIGION	117. ▶	**Moses Maimonides.**
HISTORY	118. ▶	**Chaim Herzog.**
LANGUAGE	119. ▶	**Literally "evil tongue," meaning slanderous gossip. (Jews are forbidden from engaging in it.)**
GEOGRAPHY	120. ▶	**The City of David Archeological Park.**

CURRENT
EVENTS
121. ► This conference held in Nairobi, Kenya, during the summer of 1985, rejected several anti-Zionist statements ...?

WOMEN
122. ► This wife of a Soviet Jewish prisoner has repeatedly criss-crossed the globe to plead for her husband's release...?

ARTS &
CULTURE
123. ► He was born Eugene Silverstein and starred with Zero Mostel in Mel Brooks' controversial film *The Producers*...?

PEOPLE
124. ► Which world conqueror was so kind to the Jews that many named their sons after him?

RELIGION
125. ► Which Biblical commandment is considered a "double mitzvah" if performed on the Sabbath?

HISTORY
126. ► This Jewish doctor who attended England's King Richard was also a rabbi and a philosopher...?

LANGUAGE
127. ► The word *Yiddishkeit* means...?

GEOGRAPHY
128. ► The "Good Fence" crossing point between Israel and Lebanon is located in this northern Israeli town...?

(Answers next page.)

ANSWERS

CURRENT
EVENTS

129. ► What distinguishes the Jerusalem Zoo and its unusual collection of animals from all other zoos around the world?

WOMEN

130. ► *The New York Times* called this Nobel laureate in medicine "The Madame Curie from the Bronx"....?

ARTS &
CULTURE

131. ► The Avenue of the Righteous Gentiles is located on the grounds of this world-famous Jerusalem institution...?

PEOPLE

132. ► This famous Israeli soldier-statesman once declared, "Better to keep Sharm el-Sheikh and not have peace with Egypt, than to surrender Sharm el-Sheikh and have peace"....?

RELIGION

133. ► This sinful act, according to the Talmud, is equivalent to murdering three people...?

HISTORY

134. ► This war was the outcome of an Arab policy, announced four years earlier, to weaken and destroy Israel...?

LANGUAGE

135. ► What does the Hebrew, *Am-haretz* mean?

GEOGRAPHY

136. ► The United States has been Israel's primary arms supplier since 1973. From which country did Israel acquire most of its weapons during the 1950's and 1960's...?

ANSWERS

129. ▶ It only houses animals that are referred to in the Bible.

130. ▶ Rosalyn Sussman Yalow.

131. ▶ Yad Vashem (Israel's memorial to the victims of the Holocaust).

132. ▶ Moshe Dayan.

133. ▶ Slanderous gossip. (The three victims are the speaker, the listener, and the person who was slandered.)

134. ▶ The 1956 Sinai War.

135. ▶ An ignorant Jew; a Jew who has little or no knowledge of Judaism.

136. ▶ France.

CURRENT
EVENTS

137. ► These three conditions must be met before the United States or Israel will recognize or negotiate with the PLO...?

WOMEN

138. ► What is a *sheitel*?

ARTS &
CULTURE

139. ► This non-Jewish composer and lyricist once said to his Jewish friend Richard Rogers, "The secret of my success is that I write Jewish tunes"...?

PEOPLE

140. ► In 1973 Jewish businessman Irving S. Shapiro was elected chairman and chief executive officer of this leading corporation...?

RELIGION

141. ► Among assimilated American Jews, this religious ritual above all others has become the most widely observed...?

HISTORY

142. ► In 1893, this Zionist leader suggested that the solution to the "Jewish question" was the mass conversion of Jewish children to Christianity...?

LANGUAGE

143. ► What does *Galut* mean?

GEOGRAPHY

144. ► During the Yom Kippur War, this was the only European nation which granted refueling rights to U.S. aircraft bringing military aid to Israel...?

ANSWERS

137. ► The PLO must recognize and accept Israel's right to exist. It must accept U.N. Security Council Resolutions 242 and 338, and it must desist from terrorism.

WOMEN 138. ► It's a wig worn as a head covering by Orthodox women.

ARTS & CULTURE 139. ► Cole Porter.

PEOPLE 140. ► The E.I. Du Pont de Nemours and Company.

RELIGION 141. ► Lighting Chanukah candles.

HISTORY 142. ► Theodor Herzl (This was documented in his personal diary. He later changed his mind.)

LANGUAGE 143. ► Exile, or the condition of the Jewish people in dispersion.

GEOGRAPHY 144. ► Portugal.

CURRENT
EVENTS
145. ► Name the four Jewish Republicans who currently (1985-1986) serve in the United States Senate . . . ?

WOMEN
146. ► This Jewish singer and TV personality was born Catherine Holzman . . . ?

ARTS &
CULTURE
147. ► In 1948, what Jewish organization raised more money than the American Red Cross and the United Way campaigns?

PEOPLE
148. ► He was the chairman of the Council of Economic Advisors under President Nixon and became a senior fellow at the American Enterprise Institute . . . ?

RELIGION
149. ► Which books of the Bible were the Ethiopian Jews in possession of during their isolation from the rest of world Jewry?

HISTORY
150. ► Later to become the president of a major Arab state, he was jailed in 1942 by the British for collaborating with the Nazis . . . ?

LANGUAGE
151. ► *Knaidlach*—a favorite Jewish dish is known in English as . . . ?

GEOGRAPHY
152. ► This inland sea is wholly within Israel's borders . . . ?

      (Answers next page.)

ANSWERS

CURRENT EVENTS	145. ► Sen. Rudy Boschwitz (R-Minn.), Sen. Jacob "Chic" Hecht (R-Nev.), Sen. Warren Rudman (R-N.H.), and Sen. Arlen Specter (R-Pa.).
WOMEN	146. ► Kitty Carlisle.
ARTS & CULTURE	147. ► The United Jewish Appeal Joint Campaign.
PEOPLE	148. ► Herbert Stein .
RELIGION	149. ► The first Five Books of Moses, the Book of Joshua and the Book of Ruth.
HISTORY	150. ► Anwar Sadat.
LANGUAGE	151. ► Matzah balls.
GEOGRAPHY	152. ► Lake Kinneret (also called the Sea of Galilee).

CURRENT
EVENTS

153. ▶ This writer and lecturer spoke the now-famous words "That place, Mr. President, is not your place. Your place is with the victims . . .?

WOMEN

154. ▶ In 1903 Jewish female labor activist, Rose Schneiderman, helped to organize this type of group for workers in the garment industry . . .?

ARTS &
CULTURE

155. ▶ In the early 1800's this German Jewish writer asserted: "Judaism is not a religion but a misfortune" . . .?

PEOPLE

156. ▶ This Zionist leader founded the *Haganah*, the first independent Jewish fighting force in modern times . . .?

RELIGION

157. ▶ In preparation for this holiday, many Ashkenazi Jews decorate their synagogues and homes with flowers, shrubbery and foliage, while many Sephardic Jews decorate their temple Scrolls with floral arrangements . . .?

HISTORY

158. ▶ This leading Israeli statesman was opposed to the 1981 Israeli raid on Iraq's nuclear bomb factory . . .?

LANGUAGE

159. ▶ This word means grandfather in Yiddish . . .?

GEOGRAPHY

160. ▶ In 1975, this Arab country publicly "invited" its former Jewish citizens to "return home" from Israel . . .?

(Answers next page.)

ANSWERS

53. ► Elie Wiesel, publicly urging President Reagan not to visit the German military cemetery at Bitburg.

WOMEN
154. ► A union. (It was called the United Cloth, Hat, Cap and Millinery Workers Union. She was also President of the Womens Trade Union League from 1926 to 1949.)

ARTS &
CULTURE
155. ► Heinrich Heine (who acted on his own advice and converted to Christianity).

PEOPLE
156. ► Vladimir Ze'ev Jabotinsky.

RELIGION
157. ► "Shavuos."

HISTORY
158. ► Shimon Peres.

LANGUAGE
159. ► "Zeydeh".

GEOGRAPHY
160. ► Iraq.

CURRENT
EVENTS

161. ► Which four non-Arab countries sent troops to aid the Arabs in the Yom Kippur War?

WOMEN

162. ► This Jewish television personality, famous for her interviews, originally had the family name of Volters...?

ARTS &
CULTURE

163. ► Naftali Herz Imber composed this poem in 1878. It was later set to music and became the anthem of the Zionist movement. What is it?

PEOPLE

164. ► In 1897, Hungarian-Jewish inventor David Schwarz, was asked by the German government to test his experimental transportation device. He died before the test and the device is now known by the name of the German who perfected it...?

RELIGION

165. ► Maimonides wanted Judaism to be based primarily on this principle...?

HISTORY

166. ► What did the Jordanians do to the Mount of Olives cemetery when they occupied Jerusalem?

LANGUAGE

167. ► The accusation that Jews use the blood of Christians for their religious rites, particularly in the preparation of unleavened bread for Passover, is referred to as...?

GEOGRAPHY

168. ► This Arab nation has the largest Jewish population...?

ANSWERS

161. ► Pakistan, Cuba, North Vietnam, North Korea.

162. ► Barbara Walters.

163. ► "Hatikvah", Israel's national anthem.

164. ► The Zeppelin (a blimp with a rigid metal frame, that should really be called the Schwarz).

165. ► Reason.

166. ► They built a hotel over the graves of Jewish sages desecrating the tombstones.

167. ► Blood libel.

168. ► Morocco (15,000 Jews).

CURRENT
EVENTS   169. ► General Rafael Eitan's Tehiya and Rabbi Meir Kahane's Kach are . . . ?

WOMEN   170. ► In her last acting role, Ingrid Bergman played this famous Jewish woman . . . ?

ARTS &
CULTURE   171. ► This Czech-born German novelist is the author of *The Trial, The Castle*, and *Amerika*. After his death, he was recognized as a major figure in European literature . . . ?

PEOPLE   172. ► This Jewish adviser to President Franklin D. Roosevelt coined the slogan "New Deal" . . . ?

RELIGION   173. ► One of the most significant developments of this Biblical book is the centralizing of the priestly functions in the family of Aaron and the Levites . . . ?

HISTORY   174. ► He was the first of the five Jewish Justices of the U.S. Supreme Court . . . ?

LANGUAGE   175. ► When non-Jews organize together to murder Jews and destroy Jewish property, this act is often referred to as . . . ?

GEOGRAPHY   176. ► What is the estimated world Jewish population (within 10%)?

ANSWERS

CURRENT EVENTS 169. ► Two new ultra-right-wing political parties in Israel.

WOMEN 170. ► Golda Meir.

ARTS & CULTURE 171. ► Franz Kafka.

PEOPLE 172. ► Samuel I. Rosenman.

RELIGION 173. ► Deuteronomy.

HISTORY 174. ► Louis D. Brandeis.

LANGUAGE 175. ► A pogrom.

GEOGRAPHY 176. ► 14,527,150 (according to the World Zionist Handbook).

CURRENT
EVENTS
177. ►The original charges against Klaus Barbie were for crimes against the French resistance, but these were dropped due to France's 20-year Statute of Limitation on war crimes. With what crimes will he now be charged?

WOMEN
178. ►Jessie Ethel Sampter was one of the first American women to make *aliyah* to Israel arriving after World War I. With Alexander Dushkin, what international youth movement did she bring to Palestine?

ARTS &
CULTURE
179. ►This Jewish actor-comedian was the oldest person ever to receive an Academy Award for Best Supporting Actor . . . ?

PEOPLE
180. ►When Menachem Begin was elected Prime Minister of Israel in 1977, who did he appoint as Minister of Defense?

RELIGION
181. ►The partition separating men and women in an Orthodox synagogue is called a . . . ?

HISTORY
182. ►Biographers claim that newspaper columnist Theodor Herzl first conceived the idea of Zionism after covering this infamous trial . . . ?

LANGUAGE
183. ►Why were the Dead Sea Scrolls named as such?

GEOGRAPHY
184. ►The first kibbutz in Israel, established in 1909 on the south shore of Lake Kinneret, was called . . . ?

ANSWERS

CURRENT EVENTS 177. ► Crimes against humanity, which have no statute of limitations in France. (Crimes against the Jewish people fall under this statute.)

WOMEN 178. ► The Boy Scouts or "Tsolay Tsion," (she also translated the U.S. Boy Scouts manual into Hebrew).

ARTS & CULTURE 179. ► George Burns.

PEOPLE 180. ► General Ezer Weizman.

RELIGION 181. ► "Mechitza".

HISTORY 182. ► The Alfred Dreyfus trial (in France).

LANGUAGE 183. ► They were found in a cave in Qumran, near the Dead Sea.

GEOGRAPHY 184. ► Degania.

CURRENT
EVENTS

185. ► Senator Jesse Helms of North Carolina suprised Israeli political leaders by this recent letter he wrote to President Reagan urging...?

WOMEN

186. ► This Jewish female entertainer has a mythical best friend—whom she dislikes—called Heidi Abromowitz...?

ARTS &
CULTURE

187. ► This famous Jewish songwriter and composer was born Israel Baline...?

PEOPLE

188. ► This Jewish entertainer has raised millions of dollars for the fight against muscular dystrophy...?

RELIGION

189. ► What renders a bird not kosher?

HISTORY

190. ► This ancient Hebrew's revolt resulted in a short period of Jewish independence and statehood ...?

LANGUAGE

191. ► The term *shoah* refers to ...?

GEOGRAPHY

192. ► After Jerusalem fell to the Romans, this city became a center for Talmudic study and the location of the *Sanhedrin*—the highest religious-legal tribunal of the Jews...?

      (Answers next page.)

ANSWERS

CURRENT EVENTS
185. ▶ Full, all-out U.S. aid to Israel. (Until recently, Helms had not been considered a great friend of Israel's.)

WOMEN
186. ▶ Joan Rivers.

ARTS & CULTURE
187. ▶ Irving Berlin.

PEOPLE
188. ▶ Jerry Lewis.

RELIGION
189. ▶ All birds of prey, such as eagles, are not kosher.

HISTORY
190. ▶ The Bar Kochba Revolt (in 133 C.E.).

LANGUAGE
191. ▶ The Holocaust. It literally means "terrible catastrophe."

GEOGRAPHY
192. ▶ Tiberias.

CURRENT
EVENTS

193. ► Israel's Attorney General Yitzhak
Zamir recently decided not to pro-
secute two members of the Knesset for
violating Israeli law and meeting with
this terrorist leader . . . ?

WOMEN

194. ► Elizabeth Taylor converted to Judaism
and had two Jewish husbands named
. . . ?

ARTS &
CULTURE

195. ► A.M. Rosenthal is the executive editor
of this internationally renowned
newspaper . . . ?

PEOPLE

196. ► This controversial American journalist
and playwright was a supporter of the
Irgun Zvie Leumi . . . ?

RELIGION -

197. ► Of the 613 *mitzvot* (commandments),
how many are positive command-
ments ?

HISTORY

198. ► In 1839, this Englishman proposed the
idea of establishing a Jewish State . . . ?

LANGUAGE

199. ► What is the English translation for the
Yiddish expression *prinsesen* . . . ?

GEOGRAPHY

200. ► Where is the lowest body of water on
earth . . . ?

ANSWERS

CURRENT EVENTS   193. ► Yasir Arafat.

WOMEN   194. ► Eddie Fisher and Mike Todd.

ARTS & CULTURE   195. ► The New York Times.

PEOPLE   196. ► Ben Hecht. (Because he strongly believed that the American Jewish establishment was not doing enough to assist the rescue of Europe's Jews during and after World War II.)

RELIGION   197. ► 248.

HISTORY   198. ► Sir Moses Montefiore.

LANGUAGE   199. ► A prima donna or princess.

GEOGRAPHY   200. ► The Dead Sea (1312 feet below the level of the Mediterranean Sea).

CURRENT
EVENTS

201. ► The only non-Caribbean nation which refused to condemn the United States invasion of Grenada was . . . ?

WOMEN

202. ► What is the name of the Jewish feminist magazine which calls itself "The Jewish Women's Magazine"?

ARTS &
CULTURE

203. ► This Jewish producer of nearly 300 films served for many years as National Chairman of the Anti-Defamation League of B'nai B'rith . . . ?

PEOPLE

204. ► As a youth, this U.S. Secretary of State worked in a shaving-brush factory during the day and attended New York's City College at night . . . ?

RELIGION

205. ► Why are two loaves of *challah* traditionally found on the Sabbath table?

HISTORY

206. ► Israel's "Law of Return" grants automatic citizenship to new Jewish immigrants. In what year was it enacted?

LANGUAGE

207. ► *Mitzvah* literally means . . . ?

GEOGRAPHY

208. ► The 1956 Arab-Israeli conflict erupted due to the blockade of this waterway . . . ?

ANSWERS

CURRENT EVENTS
201. ► Israel.

WOMEN
202. ► "Lilith."

ARTS & CULTURE
203. ► Dore Schary.

PEOPLE
204. ► Henry Kissinger.

RELIGION
205. ► To symbolize the double portion of "Manna" that was sent by God to feed the wandering Israelites on the Sabbath.

HISTORY
206. ► 1950.

LANGUAGE
207. ► Commandment (not charity or good deed as many think).

GEOGRAPHY
208. ► The Straits of Tiran (off the Gulf of Eilat).

CURRENT
EVENTS

209. ▶ This Israeli politician recently said, "There are no Black Jews. There are no White Jews. There are only Jews"...?

WOMEN

210. ▶ This Jewish writer was the well known restaurant critic for the *New York Times* and wrote numerous guides to fine eating...?

ARTS &
CULTURE

211. ▶ The pastry *Hamentaschen* is eaten on what Jewish holiday?

PEOPLE

212. ▶ This American Jewish mobster applied for Israeli citizenship in 1971, and was rejected...?

RELIGION

213. ▶ This Biblical figure is the hero of Deuteronomy. He transmits the Divine word, is a prophet, and intermediary, and an advocate for the Jewish people...?

HISTORY

214. ▶ The Egyptians were able to bomb Tel Aviv during only one war with Israel. Which war was it?

LANGUAGE

215. ▶ The often used phrase *Eretz Yisrael* means ...?

GEOGRAPHY

216. ▶ The small Jewish towns of Eastern Europe in which most Jews lived until the 20th Century were known as...?

ANSWERS

CURRENT EVENTS	209. ►	**Shimon Peres in a discussion about Ethiopian Jewry.**
WOMEN	210. ►	**Mimi Sheraton.**
ARTS & CULTURE	211. ►	**Purim.**
PEOPLE	212. ►	**Meyer Lansky.**
RELIGION	213. ►	**Moses.**
HISTORY	214. ►	**In 1948, the War of Independence. (At this time, Israel had no effective air force.)**
LANGUAGE	215. ►	**The Land of Israel.**
GEOGRAPHY	216. ►	**Shtetls.**

CURRENT
EVENTS

217. ► This evangelical leader called for the "Christianization" of America. After realizing that he had insulted America's Jews, he publicly apologized for his tactlessness . . . ?

WOMEN

218. ► This German born American political and social philosopher lived in France, and escaped to the U.S. in 1941. Her learned and provocative works include *The Origins of Totalitarianism* and *Eichmann in Jerusalem* . . . ?

ARTS &
CULTURE

219. ► This Jewish songwriter and musician worked as an accompanist and arranger for Marlene Dietrich. He also composed many popular hits including the musical, *Promises, Promises* and the Oscar-winning score for the movie *Butch Cassidy and the Sundance Kid* . . . ?

PEOPLE

220. ► This Yeshiva University graduate sat as judge during the Ariel Sharon vs. *Time* magazine libel trial . . . ?

RELIGION

221. ► What was the most radical of the reforms called for by the first Society of Reform Jews in America?

HISTORY

222. ► How many times has Israel captured, and then later surrendered, southern Lebanon?

LANGUAGE

223. ► What is a *minhag*?

GEOGRAPHY

224. ► Albert Einstein was offered the presidency of what country in 1952?

ANSWERS

CURRENT EVENTS	217. ►	Reverend Jerry Falwell.
WOMEN	218. ►	Hannah Arendt.
ARTS & CULTURE	219. ►	Burt Bachrach.
PEOPLE	220. ►	Judge Abraham Sofaer.
RELIGION	221. ►	The use of English during its services (it happened in Charleston, South Carolina).
HISTORY	222. ►	Three (1948, 1978 and 1982).
LANGUAGE	223. ►	A custom or tradition.
GEOGRAPHY	224. ►	Israel. (He gracefully turned down the offer.)

CURRENT
EVENTS

225. ► One of the last acts of Soviet President Konstantin Chernenko was his rejection of amnesty for this prominent Jewish *refusnick*...?

WOMEN

226. ► This female director and writer was Mike Nichols' first comedy partner ...?

ARTS &
CULTURE

227. ► Which German Jewish philosopher of anti-religious thinking said: "Where there is no reverence for the Bible, there can be no true refinement of manners"?

PEOPLE

228. ► This Jewish Pulitzer Prize-winning columnist for *The New York Times* was once an aide to President Richard Nixon...?

RELIGION

229. ► On *Shavuos*, Jews traditionally stay up all night. What is it they do during these hours?

HISTORY

230. ► This famous American politician of the Revolutionary War era said: "I will insist that Hebrews have done more to civilize men than any other nation" ...?

LANGUAGE

231. ► What does the word *kippur* in *Yom Kippur* mean?

GEOGRAPHY

232. ► In Hebrew the disputed West Bank lands are called *Yehuda* and *Shomron*. What do these names translate to in English?

ANSWERS

225. ▶ **Anatoly Shcharansky.**

226. ▶ **Elaine May.**

227. ▶ **Friedrich Nietzsche.**

228. ▶ **William Safire.**

229. ▶ **Study "Torah."**

230. ▶ **John Adams.**

231. ▶ **Atonement.**

232. ▶ **Judea and Samaria.**

CURRENT
EVENTS

233. ► In 1949, Israel voted to admit this country to the U.N. Recently, it was reported that Israeli military experts are assisting in the construction of their planes, tanks and missiles . . . ?

WOMEN

234. ► What famous woman turned into a pillar of salt because she looked back to watch the destruction of Sodom?

ARTS &
CULTURE

235. ► Which Jewish actor from the television series *Star Trek* once studied in the famous Brisk Yeshiva of Skokie, Illinois?

PEOPLE

236. ► This Jewish military leader was Secretary of the Air Force under Lyndon Johnson and Jimmy Carter's Secretary of Defense . . . ?

RELIGION

237. ► The *Mishna* and *Gemara* when combined are called . . . ?

HISTORY

238. ► Where is Babi Yar and what happened there?

LANGUAGE

239. ► What does *Megillah* mean?

GEOGRAPHY

240. ► After the 1967 Six-Day War, approximately how many times larger was the new area of Jerusalem?

ANSWERS

233. ▶ The People's Republic of China.

234. ▶ Lot's wife.

235. ▶ Leonard Nimoy.

236. ▶ Harold Brown.

237. ▶ The Talmud.

238. ▶ In Kiev, Russia. More than 30,000 Jews were killed there by the Nazis in 1941. (Recently, the Soviet Union built a housing project on the site with no memorial to commemorate the massacre.)

239. ▶ A scroll. The most famous is the Scroll of Esther read on Purim.

240. ▶ Unified Jerusalem was about three times larger than the original mandate.

CURRENT
EVENTS

241. ► This venerable American auction house sold 31 rare Hebrew books and manuscripts despite objections by Jewish organizations and the N.Y. State attorney general...?

WOMEN

242. ► This never-married Jewish feminist said, "The surest way to be alone is to get married ...?

ARTS &
CULTURE

243. ► In which Jerusalem hospital are the famous Chagall windows located?

PEOPLE

244. ► Eleazar ben Yair was a leader of these anti-Roman rebels...?

RELIGION

245. ► A common Hebrew blessing is to wish someone to live "until 120". Which Biblical figure died at that age?

HISTORY

246. ► The transmission of German Hassidism as well as other forms of German Jewish culture to Eastern Europe was largely caused by this recurring event in world history...?

LANGUAGE

247. ► When does one say *Gut yuntiff*?

GEOGRAPHY

248. ► When Britain caught Jews "illegally" immigrating to Palestine during World War II, they were sent to this country ...?

ANSWERS

CURRENT
EVENTS
241. ► Sotheby's. (Many of these rare Judaic treasures were looted by the Nazis during World War II.)

WOMEN
242. ► Gloria Steinem.

ARTS &
CULTURE
243. ► Hadassah Hospital.

PEOPLE
244. ► He commanded the Jews of Masada.

RELIGION
245. ► Moses.

HISTORY
246. ► Anti-Semitic outbreaks that forced thousands of Jews to migrate.

LANGUAGE
247. ► When wishing someone a good holiday.

GEOGRAPHY
248. ► Cyprus.

CURRENT
EVENTS

249. ► This Arab country stubbornly refuses, even today, to consider a cease-fire or armistice agreement with Israel—preferring instead to remain in a permanent state of war...?

WOMEN

250. ► This Jewish rock and roll singer had a string of hits, beginning in 1963 with her *It's my Party*...?

ARTS &
CULTURE

251. ► This English-Jewish runner and recipient of a gold medal was featured in the movie *Chariots of Fire*...?

PEOPLE

252. ► He is known as the preeminent "Nazi hunter"...?

RELIGION

253. ► This Biblical Book is a narrative of the Israelites' many years of wandering in the desert and their eventual conquest of the Promised Land...?

HISTORY

254. ► This Jewish holiday and the Warsaw Ghetto uprising occurred on the same date...?

LANGUAGE

255. ► The Hebrew word *Tzaddik* means...?

GEOGRAPHY

256. ► Twelve percent of American Jews live in these two boroughs of New York City ...?

ANSWERS

CURRENT
EVENTS

257. ► Under the terms of the current coalition government, this Israeli politician is due to succeed Shimon Peres as prime minister in 1986...?

WOMEN

258. ► It has been alleged that Golda Meir "exchanged" this Jewish underworld figure, seeking Israeli citizenship with the U.S. government in return for additional Phantom jets...?

ARTS &
CULTURE

259. ► This great Jewish author wrote the Code of Jewish Law known as the *Shulchan Aruch*...?

PEOPLE

260. ► This Jewish founder of psychoanalysis was born in Vienna in 1856 and died in London in 1939...?

RELIGION

261. ► *Yizkhor*, the Hebrew prayer for the dead, is recited in most synagogues on the last day of these three festivals...?

HISTORY

262. ► This fortress-palace near Bethlehem, built by King Herod is called...?

LANGUAGE

263. ► The Orthodox Zionist movement is popularly referred to by this name...?

GEOGRAPHY

264. ► In 1929, Arab *pogromists* murdered sixty-nine Jews in this Jewish holy city...?

ANSWERS

257. ► Deputy Premier Yitzhak Shamir.

258. ► Meyer Lansky (this was an undocumented charge).

259. ► Jospeh Caro (in the 16th century).

260. ► Sigmund Freud.

261. ► Pesach, Succos and Shavuos.

262. ► Herodion.

263. ► Mizrachi.

264. ► Hebron.

Trivia Judaica. QUESTIONS

CURRENT EVENTS
265. ► What was the code name for the 1981 Israeli mission to destroy Iraq's nuclear reactor?

WOMEN
266. ► What organization did Hannah Greenebaum Solomon found?

ARTS & CULTURE
267. ► As Israel's most famous painter, he has made original contributions to optic and kinetic art. In many of his paintings, the picture is changed by the movement of either the artwork or the viewer...?

PEOPLE
268. ► This former American citizen has served as Israeli Ambassador to Washington and as Israel's Minister of Defense...?

RELIGION
269. ► Identify three major ways that Reform and Orthodox Jews differ in their religious practices...?

HISTORY
270. ► During the 1670s, much of the Jewish world was convinced that he was the Messiah—until he converted to Islam...?

LANGUAGE
271. ► The Hebrew phrase *Shalom Bayit* means...?

GEOGRAPHY
272. ► The national flag of this Arab country was modeled after the flag of Nazi Germany...?

ANSWERS

CURRENT EVENTS
265. ▶ "Operation Babylon."

WOMEN
266. ▶ She founded the National Council of Jewish Women, the first U.S. national Jewish women's organization.

ARTS & CULTURE
267. ▶ Yaacov Agam.

PEOPLE
268. ▶ Moshe Arens.

RELIGION
269. ▶ Any of these: the use of Tefillin, the separation of men and women during prayer services, the ritual slaughtering of animals for koshering, and for men to pray with a covered head.

HISTORY
270. ▶ Shabbatai Zvi (The False Messiah).

LANGUAGE
271. ▶ Peace of the household.

GEOGRAPHY
272. ▶ Egypt.

CURRENT
EVENTS   **273.** ▶ In at least three member-states of the Arab League, slavery is still widely practiced. Name one of them . . . ?

WOMEN   **274.** ▶ This overweight Jewish rock singer was born Ellen Naomi Cohen . . . ?

ARTS &
CULTURE   **275.** ▶ This famous Conservative Rabbi's writings are modern classics of Jewish spirituality. He was well known as both an antiwar and civil rights activist . . . ?

PEOPLE   **276.** ▶ This French Jewish entertainer is considered the world's greatest mime . . . ?

RELIGION   **277.** ▶ This verb appears no fewer than 169 times in the Bible . . . ?

HISTORY   **278.** ▶ This Jewish organization was established in 1922 by the League of Nations Mandate for Palestine. It was reorganized in 1929 to encourage non-Zionist Jews to provide financial support for the creation of a Jewish homeland. It was in effect a Jewish Government even before there was a Jewish state . . . ?

LANGUAGE   **279.** ▶ The Hebrew-Yiddish word *tsurus* means . . . ?

GEOGRAPHY   **280.** ▶ This town in Israel was named after Theodor Herzl . . . ?

ANSWERS

CURRENT
EVENTS **273.** ▶ **Saudi Arabia, Algeria, Mauritania.**

WOMEN **274.** ▶ **Mama Cass Elliot.**

ARTS &
CULTURE **275.** ▶ **Abraham Joshua Heschel.**

PEOPLE **276.** ▶ **Marcel Marceau.**

RELIGION **277.** ▶ **To remember, "Zakhar."**

HISTORY **278.** ▶ **The Jewish Agency.**

LANGUAGE **279.** ▶ **Troubles.**

GEOGRAPHY **280.** ▶ **Herzliya (established in 1924).**

CURRENT EVENTS   **281.** ▶ This fundamentalist Moslem group has become a major base of terrorist activity on Israel's northern border . . . ?

WOMEN   **282.** ▶ To which royal female figure is the Sabbath often compared?

ARTS & CULTURE   **283.** ▶ This Jewish actor was the youngest ever to win an Academy Award for Best Actor, receiving it when he was 30 years old . . . ?

PEOPLE   **284.** ▶ The founder of *The New Republic* magazine, a Pulitzer Prize winning American Jewish journalist, was the most influential pundit of his era . . . ?

RELIGION   **285.** ▶ The Talmud dictates that this type of person takes precedence over a king . . . ?

HISTORY   **286.** ▶ The *Palmach* organization was created before the establishment of the State of Israel. Why was it formed?

LANGUAGE   **287.** ▶ What does the word *goy* mean?

GEOGRAPHY   **288.** ▶ In what country was Adolf Eichmann captured and where was he brought to trial?

     (Answers next page.)

ANSWERS

CURRENT EVENTS **281.** ► **The Shiite Moslems.**

WOMEN **282.** ► **A queen.**

ARTS & CULTURE **283.** ► **Richard Dreyfus.**

PEOPLE **284.** ► **Walter Lippmann.**

RELIGION **285.** ► **The scholar.**

HISTORY **286.** ► **To provide the Haganah with a reserve of crack soldiers always ready for special military missions against the enemies of Israel.**

LANGUAGE **287.** ► **"Nation," although it is often used in a pejorative sense to refer to an individual who is not Jewish.**

GEOGRAPHY **288.** ► **He was captured in Argentina, and brought to trial in Israel.**

CURRENT
EVENTS

289. ► A recent Israeli public opinion poll revealed that as many as forty percent of secondary-school pupils support this ultra-nationalist Israeli politician . . . ?

WOMEN

290. ► Theodosia Goodman was the original name of this Jewish silent screen star . . . ?

ARTS &
CULTURE

291. ► This Jewish singing duo started out with the stage names of Tom and Jerry, but later returned to their original names, which were . . . ?

PEOPLE

292. ► This English philanthropist provided the funds for the construction of the Israeli Knesset . . . ?

RELIGION

293. ► These characteristics identify a fish that is kosher . . . ?

HISTORY

294. ► Name two of the first three nations that formally recognized the State of Israel in 1948 . . . ?

LANGUAGE

295. ► Israel's General Federation of Jewish Labor, founded in December 1920, is called . . . ?

GEOGRAPHY

296. ► Which three American states have the largest Jewish populations . . . ?

(Answers next page.)

ANSWERS

CURRENT
EVENTS   **289.** ► **Rabbi Meir Kahane.**

WOMEN   **290.** ► **Theda Bara.**

ARTS &
CULTURE   **291.** ► **Simon and Garfunkel.**

PEOPLE   **292.** ► **James R. Rothschild.**

RELIGION   **293.** ► **A fish must have both fins and scales.**

HISTORY   **294.** ► **The United States, the Soviet Union
                              and Nicaragua.**

LANGUAGE   **295.** ► **The "Histadrut."**

GEOGRAPHY   **296.** ► **New York, New Jersey and Florida
                              (Washington, D.C. would be second if
                              it were a state).**

CURRENT EVENTS

297. ► Arch anti-Semite, Louis Farrakhan, received a five million dollar "loan" from this government in 1985 . . . ?

WOMEN

298. ► This Jewish columnist was born Sylvia Field Feldman, but is known today as . . . ?

ARTS & CULTURE

299. ► Yehuda Halevi was accomplished in this field of the arts . . . ?

PEOPLE

300. ► This statesman was the first Israeli Ambassador to the United States . . . ?

RELIGION

301. ► State in English the first line of the *shema*, the Jewish confession of faith which is recited daily . . . ?

HISTORY

302. ► He established a dynasty which lasted 400 years until the Babylonian conquest. He unified the southern and northern tribes, and made Jerusalem his capital . . . ?

LANGUAGE

303. ► This language was developed by the Ashkenazim . . . ?

GEOGRAPHY

304. ► The Israeli settlement of Mei-Ami was formed in 1963 with donations from American Jews. The story behind the origin of its name is . . . ?

(Answers next page.)

ANSWERS

CURRENT
EVENTS

297. ► Libya. (He claims that the money will be used to improve the economic status of blacks in the U.S.)

WOMEN

298. ► Sylvia Porter.

ARTS &
CULTURE

299. ► Poetry.

PEOPLE

300. ► Abba Eban.

RELIGION

301. ► "Hear O Israel the Lord is Our God, the Lord is One."

HISTORY

302. ► King David (1004 BCE to 960 BCE).

LANGUAGE

303. ► Yiddish.

GEOGRAPHY

304. ► Jews from Miami, Florida donated the money to start this settlement and the Israeli government decided to Hebraize the name of the donors home town. (It means waters of my nation.)

ANSWERS

CURRENT EVENTS **305.** ► Menachem Z. Rosensaft, chairman of the International Network of Children of Jewish Holocuast Survivors, recently accused these two American agencies of withholding critical information regarding Dr. Josef Mengele?

WOMEN **306.** ► This Jewish actress was born Shirley Schrift . . . ?

ARTS & CULTURE **307.** ► Who played the role of Ari Ben-Canaan in *Exodus*, the noted movie about Israel's early modern history . . . ?

PEOPLE **308.** ► For the first ten years of her career, this financial columnist and author wrote a column whose byline did not disclose her sex . . . ?

RELIGION **309.** ► Which food is used as a dip on Rosh Hashanah, to symbolize the sweetness of the coming year?

HISTORY **310.** ► Israel was formally proclaimed a state at 4 o'clock in the afternoon on this date . . . ?

LANGUAGE **311.** ► The period when modern European culture was spread among the Jewish people is referred to as the *Haskalah* and means . . . ?

GEOGRAPHY **312.** ► The combined Jewish population of Europe is (within ten percent accuracy) . . . ?

77 (Answers next page.)

ANSWERS

CURRENT
EVENTS

313. ▶ According to recent public opinion surveys, most European-born Ashkenazi Jews tend to vote for this Israeli political party . . . ?

WOMEN

314. ▶ This still glamorous actress was known as "The Look" at the beginning of her movie career . . . ?

ARTS &
CULTURE

315. ▶ This Jewish comedian and member of the Marx Brothers team was born Adolph Marx, but was known by the stage name . . . ?

PEOPLE

316. ▶ This university professor and 1970 Nobel Prize winner in economics wrote the most widely used textbook on economics . . . ?

RELIGION

317. ▶ This Biblical Prophet attends every circumcision to protect the Jewish infant from danger . . . ?

HISTORY

318. ▶ How many times has Israel captured the Straits of Tiran from Egypt?

LANGUAGE

319. ▶ Russian Jews who attempt to leave their country but are prevented from doing so by their government are referred to by this hybrid English word . . . ?

GEOGRAPHY

320. ▶ This European Jewish community plays a key role in the diamond trade and is the most Orthodox in Europe . . . ?

ANSWERS

CURRENT
EVENTS   313. ▶ **The Labor Party.**

WOMEN   314. ▶ **Lauren Bacall.**

ARTS &
CULTURE   315. ▶ **Harpo.**

PEOPLE   316. ▶ **Professor Paul Samuelson.**

RELIGION   317. ▶ **Elijah.**

HISTORY   318. ▶ **Twice: First, during the Sinai Campaign of 1956. (Israel captured the Straits which had been used by Egypt to hinder navigation since 1948.) Second, during the 1967 Six-Day War. (Egypt seized the Straits with the express purpose of stopping Israel's traffic. (Israel retaliated and the Six-Day War began.)**

LANGUAGE   319. ▶ **"Refuseniks".**

GEOGRAPHY 320. ▶ **Antwerp, Belgium.**

CURRENT
EVENTS

321. ► This former Defense Minister, ran for Prime Minister of Israel three times, losing twice . . . ?

WOMEN

322. ► Who was Beruryah and what was unique about her?

ARTS &
CULTURE

323. ► This Jewish comedian made his film debut in the movie *What's New Pussycat* . . . ?

PEOPLE

324. ► How many Marx Brothers were there?

RELIGION

325. ► Why is a *mezuzah* fixed to the doorpost in a Jewish home?

HISTORY

326. ► Since the creation of the world, the largest and most dense concentration of Jews has been in this area . . . ?

LANGUAGE

327. ► The song, *Bei Mir Bista Shein*, was the most financially successful Yiddish song of all time. In English it is known as . . . ?

GEOGRAPHY

328. ► This continent has the largest number of Jewish inhabitants . . . ?

ANSWERS

CURRENT EVENTS

321. ► 1984. Current Prime Minister Shimon Peres was finally elected Prime Minister of a National Unity Government.

WOMEN

322. ► She was the daughter of Rabbi Hanina ben Teradyon and the only female Talmudist of her time.

ARTS & CULTURE

323. ► Woody Allen.

PEOPLE

324. ► Five.

RELIGION

325. ► Because it is prescribed by the Commandment stating: "Thou shalt write them (the Ten Commandments) upon the doorposts of thy house..."

HISTORY

326. ► The New York Metropolitan area.

LANGUAGE

327. ► For Me You Are Beautiful.

GEOGRAPHY

328. ► North America (est. 6,360,000).

CURRENT
EVENTS

329. ► What is the *Gadna* program that all Israeli high school students are required to enroll in . . . ?

WOMEN

330. ► This Jewish woman was the manager of a famous family hotel in the Catskill Mountains and wrote her own cookbook . . . ?

ARTS &
CULTURE

331. ► This Jewish author reportedly failed English in high school, but later wrote the bestselling novel, *Exodus* . . . ?

PEOPLE

332. ► This Jewish athlete holds the world's record for winning the most gold medals in a single Olympics . . . ?

RELIGION

333. ► What do Sephardic Jews call their most learned rabbis?

HISTORY

334. ► Which act of defiance sparked the Maccabean Revolt which *Chanukah* commemorates?

LANGUAGE

335. ► The difference between *kvetch* and *kvitch* is . . . ?

GEOGRAPHY

336. ► In the 19th century, in this country, there were mass conversions of Jews to Christianity . . . ?

        (Answers next page.)

ANSWERS

CURRENT
EVENTS
329. ► **The mandatory pre-military training. (It stands for "Ghedudei Naor" or Youth Troops.)**

WOMEN
330. ► **Jennie Grossinger.**

ARTS &
CULTURE
331. ► **Leon Uris.**

PEOPLE
332. ► **Mark Spitz.**

RELIGION
333. ► **"Hachamin," or sages.**

HISTORY
334. ► **The refusal of the Maccabees to submit to the Greeks' demand that they publicly eat pork.**

LANGUAGE
335. ► **The former means "to complain," the latter—"to squeal.".**

GEOGRAPHY
336. ► **Germany.**

CURRENT
EVENTS
337. ► This outspoken Israeli leader recently accused the Labor party of not knowing how to "Stand up to the gentiles" ...?

WOMEN
338. ► She was the Prophetess that led the Israelites in dancing and praising God—after they escaped from Egypt ...?

ARTS &
CULTURE
339. ► This Jewish author originally published the book *The Education of Hyman Kaplan*, using the pen name Leonard Q. Ross...?

PEOPLE
340. ► During the British rule of Palestine, this Jewish politician was the first High Commissioner...?

RELIGION
341. ► Why is it customary for the groom to wear a *kittel* at a traditional Jewish wedding?

HISTORY
342. ► When the Romans conquered the Land of Israel, they changed its name to...?

LANGUAGE
343. ► What are the common Hebrew words for the Jewish concepts of forbidden and permitted food?

GEOGRAPHY
344. ► Which Arab country has a law barring Jews from ever entering it?

(Answers next page.)

ANSWERS

337. ► **Ariel Sharon, minister of commerce and industry. (He was commenting on the Labor government's response to President Reagan's trip to Bitburg.)**

338. ► **Miriam (the sister of Moses).**

339. ► **Leo Rosten.**

340. ► **Sir Herbert Samuel.**

341. ► **The white robe is a symbol of purity and rebirth.**

342. ► **Palestine.**

343. ► **"Kosher" and "Trefah."**

344. ► **Saudi Arabia.**

CURRENT
EVENTS
345. ► What did Wisconsin's Senator Bob Kasten recently do to insure that the U.N. would not be used as a tool of anti-Semitic forces without suffering severe financial penalties?

WOMEN
346. ► Born in 1867, this Jewish woman was active in social work and founded the Henry Street Settlement...?

ARTS &
CULTURE
347. ► Which Jewish genius directed this 1984 humor film about a hopeless theatrical agent who was a total loser?

PEOPLE
348. ► This impresario presented artists such as Isadora Duncan, Arthur Rubinstein and Anna Pavlova. He also brought the Bolshoi Ballet to the U.S....?

RELIGION
349. ► This Jewish holiday stresses among other things the principle of liberty...?

HISTORY
350. ► Which famous Zionist leader was buried in Vienna in 1904 but reinterred on Jerusalem's Mount Herzl in 1949?

LANGUAGE
351. ► The Yiddish word *umgelumpert* refers to one who is ...?

GEOGRAPHY
352. ► In which country did the miracle of *Chanukah* occur?

          (Answers next page.)

ANSWERS

CURRENT EVENTS

345. ▶ He successfully introduced legislation that imposes permanent financial penalties on any U.N. agency that deprives Israel of its rights. (The offending agencies would lose the U.S. contribution of 25% of its budgets.)

WOMEN

346. ▶ Lillian Wald.

ARTS & CULTURE

347. ▶ Woody Allen, directing "Broadway Danny Rose."

PEOPLE

348. ▶ Sol Hurok.

RELIGION

349. ▶ Passover. (It commemorates when the Jewish slaves in Egypt gained their freedom.)

HISTORY

350. ▶ Theodor Herzl.

LANGUAGE

351. ▶ Awkward.

GEOGRAPHY

352. ▶ In the country that is now Israel.

CURRENT EVENTS

353. ► Name the only two Jews who have been elected Mayor of New York City ...?

WOMEN

354. ► This Jewish woman is Chairman of the Board of the *Washingvton Post Company*...?

ARTS & CULTURE

355. ► Among his most popular books, this late Israeli soldier-statesman wrote *Diary of The Sinai Campaign, Living with the Bible, Breakthrough* and his autobiography, *The Story of My Life* ...?

PEOPLE

356. ► What portion of world Jewry perished during the Nazi Holocaust?

RELIGION

357. ► He founded the Jewish Reconstructionist Movement in 1922...?

HISTORY

358. ► This Jewish politician was elected governor of New York after Franklin D. Roosevelt...?

LANGUAGE

359. ► The Yiddish equivalent of the Italian *ravioli* are...?

GEOGRAPHY

360. ► In Jerusalem, on *Shavuos*, it is the custom for Jews to meet at this location at sunrise for the morning prayer service...?

(Answers next page.)

ANSWERS

CURRENT
EVENTS
353. ► Abraham Beame and Edward I. Koch.

WOMEN
354. ► Katherine Graham.

ARTS &
CULTURE
355. ► Moshe Dayan.

PEOPLE
356. ► One third of the Jewish people.

RELIGION
357. ► Dr. Mordecai Kaplan. (Their religious services are similiar to those of the Conservative Movement).

HISTORY
358. ► Herbert Lehman.

LANGUAGE
359. ► "Kreplach."

GEOGRAPHY
360. ► The Western Wall. (It is also known as the kotel.)

CURRENT
EVENTS

361. ► When the communist Sandinistas seized power in Nicaragua what did they do to Israel's Embassy . . . ?

WOMEN

362. ► This Biblical book, named after a woman, is a love story . . . ?

ARTS &
CULTURE

363. ► Born Ya'akov Moshe Maze, this former rabbi has become well known as a comedian whose trademark is his heavy Jewish accent . . . ?

PEOPLE

364. ► This would-be *Messiah* was asked to choose between death and the Moslem faith and, to the horror of hundreds of thousands of his followers, he chose to don the turban . . . ?

RELIGION

365. ► *Kiddush* is said on . . . ?

HISTORY

366. ► In what month is "Holocaust Remembrance Day"?

LANGUAGE

367. ► The yiddish word *kibbitz* means . . . ?

GEOGRAPHY

368. ► Jesus was born a Jew in this town . . . ?

ANSWERS

CURRENT EVENTS

361. ► They turned it over to the P.L.O. (They also closed all synagogues, confiscated property and valuables, and expelled the country's Jews.)

WOMEN

362. ► The Book of Ruth.

ARTS & CULTURE

363. ► Jackie Mason.

PEOPLE

364. ► Shabatai Zvi, the False Messiah.

RELIGION

365. ► The Sabbath and holidays. (It is a prayer recited over a cup of wine.)

HISTORY

366. ► April (19th).

LANGUAGE

367. ► To offer unwanted advice as a talkative bystander in a game would.

GEOGRAPHY

368. ► Bethlehem.

CURRENT
EVENTS
369. ► Before the Holocaust, over three-and-a half million Jews lived in Poland. How many live there today (within 10% accuracy)?

WOMEN
370. ► This Dutch Jewish girl is known throughout the world for the writing she did while hiding from the Nazis in Amsterdam . . . ?

ARTS &
CULTURE
371. ► This Jewish comedian and member of the Marx Brothers team was born Herbert Marx but was known by his stage name . . . ?

PEOPLE
372. ► The American brother of this right wing Israeli politician is a U.S. professor. He is outspoken on behalf of Arab causes and once publicly compared Israel to Nazi Germany . . . ?

RELIGION
373. ► According to the Story of Creation, what existed on the first day of the world?

HISTORY
374. ► Before World War I Jewish financiers refused to make loans to this government . . . ?

LANGUAGE
375. ► This traditional Jewish food is a baked or fried roll of dough usually filled with mashed potato or meat . . . ?

GEOGRAPHY
376. ► Lake Kinneret, in northern Israel, is commonly referred to by this name . . . ?

(Answers next page.)

ANSWERS

CURRENT EVENTS **369.** ▶ **About 5,000 remain. (The virulent anti-Semitism of the Polish population lingered on even after the Holocaust, inspiring the remaining Jews to resettle elsewhere.**

WOMEN **370.** ▶ **Anne Frank.**

ARTS & CULTURE **371.** ▶ **Zeppo.**

PEOPLE **372.** ▶ **Moshe Arens. (His brother is Richard Arens.)**

RELIGION **373.** ▶ **Light and darkness.**

HISTORY **374.** ▶ **The Soviet Union because of the murderous pogroms encouraged by the Russian government.**

LANGUAGE **375.** ▶ **A knish.**

GEOGRAPHY **376.** ▶ **The Sea of Galilee.**

CURRENT
EVENTS

377. ► Israel has been refused membership in the International Red Cross because . . . ?

WOMEN

378. ► What item must an Orthodox Jewish woman have in her possession or know the exact whereabouts of—in order to live with her husband?

ARTS &
CULTURE

379. ► This Jewish writer won the 1976 Pulitzer Prize for Fiction for his book, *The Fixer* . . . ?

PEOPLE

380. ► He founded the Zionist Youth Movement, *Betar*, in 1923 . . . ?

RELIGION

381. ► Why does the pious Jew believe that he should always cover his head as a sign of respect for God?

HISTORY

382. ► Enacted by the Knesset in 1950, this law grants automatic Israeli citizenship to Jewish immigrants . . . ?

LANGUAGE

383. ► The Yiddish expression *kochleffel* means . . . ?

GEOGRAPHY

383. ► This holy city in Israel was King David's first capital . . . ?

ANSWERS

377. ▶ Official reason: The only two symbols
recognized by the Red Cross are the
Cross and the Crescent—the Star of
David is not acceptable and since Israel
uses this symbol she cannot be a
member.
Real reason: The 21 Arab states that
belong have threatened to withdraw if
Israel is allowed to join.

WOMEN 378. ▶ The "ketubah," or Jewish marriage
contract.

ARTS &
CULTURE 379. ▶ Bernard Malamud.

PEOPLE 380. ▶ Vladimir Ze'ev Jabotinsky.

RELIGION 381. ▶ He considers himself always standing
before God.

HISTORY 382. ▶ The Law of Return.

LANGUAGE 383. ▶ One who stirs up trouble. (Literally:
cooking spoon.)

GEOGRAPHY 384. ▶ Hebron.

CURRENT EVENTS

385. ► What is unusual about the ethnic background of President Reagan's Cabinet and senior White House staff?

WOMEN

386. ► This 1983 Jewish-theme film has been called "the most lavish film ever to feature a Jewish female leading role" . . .?

ARTS & CULTURE

387. ► He was born Leonard Rosenberg and was the fastidious half of a popular TV situation comedy adapted from a successful movie . . .?

PEOPLE

388. ► This Jewish entrepreneur invented the Polaroid camera . . .?

RELIGION

389. ► What are the *aidim* at traditional Jewish marriage ceremonies supposed to witness?

HISTORY

390. ► How was Israeli super-spy Eli Cohen discovered . . .?

LANGUAGE

391. ► The Russian word for "devastation" is a derivative of this term that unfortunately describes what frequently happened to Russian Jews during and prior to WW I and WW II . . .?

GEOGRAPHY

392. ► It is alleged that this African country has assisted Israel's development of nuclear weapons . . .?

ANSWERS

CURRENT
EVENTS
385. ▶ He is the first President in recent times to have no Jews represented in any high-ranking positions.

WOMEN
386. ▶ "Yentl" (directed by and starring Barbra Streisand).

ARTS &
CULTURE
387. ▶ Tony Randall (as Felix Unger in "The Odd Couple").

PEOPLE
388. ▶ Edward Land.

RELIGION
389. ▶ The signing of the "ketuba" or marriage contract.

HISTORY
390. ▶ The Soviet Union had provided Syria with advanced electronic surveillance equipment that uncovered Cohen's secret radio transmissions to Israel.

LANGUAGE
391. ▶ "Pogroms." (The organized devastation of Jewish life and property by anti-Semites.)

GEOGRAPHY
392. ▶ South Africa.

CURRENT
EVENTS

393. ► What was Elie Wiesel's official purpose for being in Washington, D.C. in May, 1985 and publicly speaking to President Reagan before the world press?

WOMEN

394. ► In the 1920s, Jewish political analyst, Belle Moskowitz, was the liberal advisor to one of the most prominent politicians in the United States. Who was he?

ARTS &
CULTURE

395. ► Yigael Yadin, Israel's second Chief of Staff, later became a leading Israeli scientist in this field and made several major discoveries. . . ?

PEOPLE

396. ► What famous Jewish baseball player, the youngest (26) ever elected to the Hall of Fame, refused to play on *Rosh Hashana* and *Yom Kippur*?

RELIGION

397. ► What is the greatest irony concerning the debate ranging over the issue of non-Orthodox conversions to Judaism and the fact that these converts cannot be guaranteed automatic registration as Jews on the books of the Israeli rabbinate. . . ?

HISTORY

398. ► The 1956 Egyptian-Israeli War is more commonly referred to as. . . ?

LANGUAGE

399. ► The Yiddish word *haimish* literally means. . . ?

GEOGRAPHY

400. ► This Biblical place was described in the book of Zechariah as the "City of Peace and Truth". . . ?

99   (Answers next page.)

ANSWERS

CURRENT
EVENTS
393. ► **To receive the Congressional Gold Medal of Achievement. (He attempted to persaude President Reagan not to visit Bitburg, the German military cemetery where Nazi officers are buried.)**

WOMEN
394. ► **Alfred E. Smith, (Governor of New York).**

ARTS &
CULTURE
395. ► **Archaelogy (he explored Hazor and Masada).**

PEOPLE
396. ► **Sandy Koufax.**

RELIGION
397. ► **The average number of converts that apply for "aliyah" from the U.S. averages only 6 per year.**

HISTORY
398. ► **The Sinai Campaign.**

LANGUAGE
399. ► **Friendly and down-to-earth.**

GEOGRAPHY
400. ► **Jerusalem.**

CURRENT
EVENTS
401. ► In 1985, the United States Supreme Court decided to hear the case dealing with whether an observant Jew could wear this forbidden religious garb while serving in the armed forces . . . ?

WOMEN
402. ► The *Bat Mitzvah* ceremony for females originated within this Jewish movement . . . ?

ARTS &
CULTURE
403. ► This renowned Jewish astronomer won a Pulitzer Prize in 1978 for his book *The Dragons of Eden* . . . ?

PEOPLE
404. ► This Israeli spy working in Damascus managed to become the top aide to the Syrian defense minister, before he was uncovered and executed in 1965 . . . ?

RELIGION
405. ► What does *maror* symbolize at the Passover Seder?

HISTORY
406. ► This late Egyptian leader repeatedly referred to *The Protocols of the Elders of Zion* to document his charge that three hundred Zionists ruled the world . . . ?

LANGUAGE
407. ► This garment is called *gatkes* . . . ?

GEOGRAPHY
408. ► The first Jewish astronaut was a citizen of this nation . . . ?

(Answers next page.)

ANSWERS

CURRENT
EVENTS **401.** ► A "yarmulke".

WOMEN **402.** ► The Reconstructionist (in 1922).

ARTS &
CULTURE **403.** ► Dr. Carl Sagan.

PEOPLE **404.** ► Eli Cohen.

RELIGION **405.** ► This bitter herb represents the bitter life of the Jewish slaves.

HISTORY **406.** ► Gamel Abdul Nasser.

LANGUAGE **407.** ► Long johns.

GEOGRAPHY **408.** ► The USSR (Boris Volynov).

CURRENT
EVENTS
409. ► In the summer of 1985, the rate of exchange of American dollars to Israeli shekels was fixed by the Israeli government at this rate . . . ?

WOMEN
410. ► The stage name of the blonde Jewish actress, born Judith Turim, who starred in *Bells Are Ringing* and *Born Yesterday*—is based on the English translation of her Hebrew surname . . . ?

ARTS &
CULTURE
411. ► This Jewish comedian said, "I don't want to belong to any club that accepts people like me as members" . . . ?

PEOPLE
412. ► In 1970, this United Nations envoy unsuccessfully sought to negotiate a peace treaty between Israel and Egypt . . . ?

RELIGION
413. ► The longest book of the Torah is . . . ?

HISTORY
414. ► One of the first acts of Iran's Ayatollah Khomeini after he asumed power was the takeover of . . . ?

LANGUAGE
415. ► What is the meaning of the Hebrew greeting *Shavua Tov*, used after the conclusion of the Sabbath?

GEOGRAPHY
416. ► This European nation has the largest number of Jewish citizens . . . ?

 (Answers next page.)

ANSWERS

409. ► 1500 shekels to the dollar. (This move was a devaluation to stabilize the downward spiral of the shekel's value.)

WOMEN 410. ► Judy Holliday.

ARTS &
CULTURE 411. ► Groucho Marx.

PEOPLE 412. ► Gunnar Jarring.

RELIGION 413. ► Genesis.

HISTORY 414. ► The Israeli embassy in Tehran.

LANGUAGE 415. ► "Have a good week."

GEOGRAPHY 416. ► France (est. 650,000).

CURRENT
EVENTS

417. ▶ The Israeli government refers to the 1982 war in Lebanon by this alternative English name . . . ?

WOMEN

418. ▶ This 1967 movie, starring a Jewish female, signaled a new pride in being Jewish. The star was playing up her heritage instead of avoiding it . . . ?

ARTS &
CULTURE

419. ▶ He was the most famous Jewish actor in *The Wizard of Oz*, playing the role of a not-so-wild animal . . . ?

PEOPLE

420. ▶ This Jewish hero lost his life while defending the northern settlement of Tel Hai against Arab attackers in 1920. His immortal last words were "No matter; it is good to die for our country" . . . ?

RELIGION

421. ▶ On which holiday is it customary in some Jewish homes to serve a cooked fish-head with the meal . . . ?

HISTORY

422. ▶ He was the President of the United States when America recognized the new State of Israel . . . ?

LANGUAGE

423. ▶ The much overused Yiddish expression, *maven*, refers to . . . ?

GEOGRAPHY

424. ▶ In 1972, world attention focused on 31 Connallystrasse Street in Munich because of this notorious event . . . ?

ANSWERS

417. ▶ "Operation Peace for Galilee".

418. ▶ "Funny Girl," starring Barbra Streisand. She played the Jewish Fanny Brice.

419. ▶ Bert Lahr (the Cowardly Lion).

420. ▶ Joseph Trumpeldor.

421. ▶ Rosh Hashanah (it symbolically represents the 'head' of the year).

422. ▶ Harry S. Truman.

423. ▶ An expert (it comes form the Hebrew "he who understands").

424. ▶ It was the living quarters of the Israeli athletes at the Olympic Village, who were taken hostage and murdered by PLO terrorists.

CURRENT EVENTS

425. ► Why did President Carter's liaison to the Jewish community, Mark Siegel, resign his post in 1978?

WOMEN

426. ► What is a *tichel*?

ARTS & CULTURE

427. ► This Australian writer won Britain's prestigious Booker Literary Prize for his book *Schindler's List* which was about Oskar Schindler's rescue of over 900 Jews during World War II . . . ?

PEOPLE

428. ► As prime minister, Menachem Begin presented this Christian minister with an award as the non-Israeli "Man of the Year" . . . ?

RELIGION

429. ► What is another name for the eighth day of Tabernacles?

HISTORY

430. ► This former army paratrooper was the first Israeli-born Ambassador to the United Nations . . . ?

LANGUAGE

431. ► One who thinks like a smart Jewish person is a . . . ?

GEOGRAPHY

432. ► Moses Maimonides was the personal physician to the royal family of this country . . . ?

(Answers next page.)

ANSWERS

CURRENT
EVENTS

425. ► To protest the Administration's sale of F-15 fighter aircraft to Saudia Arabia.

WOMEN

426. ► A kerchief which Orthodox women use to cover their hair, in accordance with Jewish law.

ARTS &
CULTURE

427. ► Thomas Keneally (who is not Jewish).

PEOPLE

428. ► Reverend Jerry Falwell (in a controversial award decision).

RELIGION

429. ► "Sh'mini Atzereth" or the Eighth Day of Assembly. (It marks the close of the festival.)

HISTORY

430. ► Benjamin Netanyahu.

LANGUAGE

431. ► "Yiddishe kop."

GEOGRAPHY

432. ► Egypt.

CURRENT
EVENTS

433. ▶ The Arabs have surpassed Israel technologically in this one area...?

WOMEN

434. ▶ In 1980, President Jimmy Carter presented this world-renowned Jewish opera star with the Presidential Medal of Freedom...?

ARTS &
CULTURE

435. ▶ What was unique about the boxing shorts worn by Jewish boxer Max Baer?

PEOPLE

436. ▶ He was known as the "Prophet of the State of Israel"...?

RELIGION

437. ▶ In this Book of the Bible, the concept of monotheism is central and emphasized repeatedly...?

HISTORY

438. ▶ In this European country, synagogues and Jewish cultural organizations are never considered as tax-exempt institutions, rabbis are not excused from military service and the rabbinate, when offering legal testimony, enjoys no rights of confidentiality in matters relating to the Jewish ministry...?

LANGUAGE

439. ▶ He is considered the father of modern Hebrew...?

GEOGRAPHY

440. ▶ Israeli citizens are required to pay a $300 travel tax each time they leave the country. How do Arabs who are Israeli citizens avoid paying this tax?

ANSWERS

CURRENT EVENTS **433.** ► Placing communications satellites in space. (This was accomplished during the recent flight of a Saudi Arabian prince on a U.S. space shuttle mission.)

WOMEN **434.** ► Beverly Sills.

ARTS & CULTURE **435.** ► The Star of David was sewn on them.

PEOPLE **436.** ► Theodor Herzl.

RELIGION **437.** ► Deuteronomy.

HISTORY **438.** ► Spain. (A new set of laws to grant rabbis the same privileges enjoyed by priests is under review and may be approved this year.)

LANGUAGE **439.** ► Eliezer Ben Yehuda.

GEOGRAPHY **440.** ► They leave Israel via Jordan.

CURRENT
EVENTS   **441.** ► The U.S. Senate has recently revoked the American funding of these U.N. Agencies, because of their anti-Israel and anti-Semitic behavior . . . ?

WOMEN   **442.** ► Golda Meir's first political post in the State of Israel was . . . ?

ARTS &
CULTURE   **443.** ► Amos Oz, A.B. Yehoshua, Amos Elon and Yehuda Amichai all share this distinction . . . ?

PEOPLE   **444.** ► This Jewish jurist was appointed to the Supreme Court in 1965, and resigned in 1969 . . . ?

RELIGION   **445.** ► Why is *Yom Kippur* eve the only time Jews wear *talit* in the evening?

HISTORY   **446.** ► In 1825, Mordecai Manuel Noah attempted to establish a homeland for European Jews to be called Ararat—in this part of the United States . . . ?

LANGUAGE   **447.** ► This commonly used English term was coined in 1879 by Wilhelm Marr, a notorious despiser of Jews, as a euphemistic substitute for "Jew-hater" . . . ?

GEOGRAPHY   **448.** ► These Biblical rivers, *Pishon, Tigni, Givon and Euphrates* all flowed in this the general vicinity of this well-known Biblical location . . . ?

ANSWERS

CURRENT EVENTS **441.** ► The Committee on Elimination of Racial Discrimination, The Committee on the Exercise of the Inalienable Rights of the Palestinian People, The Special Unit on Palestine Rights and Projects.

WOMEN **442.** ► Israel's Ambassador to the Soviet Union.

ARTS & CULTURE **443.** ► They are widely acclaimed and widely translated Israeli writers.

PEOPLE **444.** ► The Hon. Abe Fortas.

RELIGION **445.** ► Because all of "Yom Kippur" is considered to be part of one day. Thus, the "talit," which can only be worn during daylight hours, is appropriate.

HISTORY **446.** ► In New York State. (He proposed that the settlement be on Grant Island off the Niagara River. The U.S. government rejected the proposal.)

LANGUAGE **447.** ► Anti-Semitism.

GEOGRAPHY **448.** ► The Garden of Eden.

CURRENT
EVENTS

449. ► Anwar Sadat called him the most famous mayor in the world...?

WOMEN

450. ► This leading Jewish feminist leader was born Betty Naomi Goldstein...?

ARTS &
CULTURE

451. ► The Jewish creator of Paramount Pictures, Adolph Zukor, founded another type of entertainment that is still widely popular but now costs about twenty-five times more than it did originally...?

PEOPLE

452. ► This assimilated Jewish psychiatrist and social critic began working with Theodor Herzl in 1895 and went on to become a co-founder of the World Zionist Organization...?

RELIGION

453. ► On the first day of *Rosh Hashanah* 5726, in 1965, what Jewish event occured in a historic Washington, D.C. government building...?

HISTORY

454. ► For what political achievement is Zalman Shazar most noted?

LANGUAGE

455. ► The abbreviation for the Jewish "Organization for Vocational Training" is...?

GEOGRAPHY

456. ► In which part of the world did most of the Jewish schools known as *Cheders* operate?

ANSWERS

449. ► Teddy Kollek of Jerusalem.

450. ► Betty Friedan.

451. ► The Penny Arcade.

452. ► Dr. Max Nordau.

453. ► A High Holy Day service was held in the United States Capitol Building.

454. ► He served as President of the State of Israel (from 1963 to 1973).

455. ► O.R.T.

456. ► Eastern Europe.

CURRENT
EVENTS   **457.** ► This country granted Israel $2.5 billion in military and economic assistance in fiscal year 1985...?

WOMEN   **458.** ► Jacob had twelve sons and one daughter. What was her name?

ARTS &
CULTURE   **459.** ► In his autobiography, *For the Life of Me*, this famous Irish Jew writes about how he helped teach guerrilla warfare tactics to members of the Palestine Jewish underground group, the *Irgun Zvie Leumi*...?

PEOPLE   **460.** ► This mass-murderer was in charge of implementing Hitler's "Final Solution"?

RELIGION   **461.** ► According to Jewish law, which is preferable to use in a *Chanukah menorah*—candles or oil?

HISTORY   **462.** ► These two nations had the largest Jewish communities during Medieval times...?

LANGUAGE   **463.** ► This Jewish word means both righteousness and charity...?

GEOGRAPHY   **464.** ► Which contemporary Arab capitals were once part of ancient Israel?

         (Answers next page.)

ANSWERS

457. ► **The United States.**

458. ► **Dinah.**

459. ► **Robert Briscoe (the former mayor of Dublin, Ireland).**

460. ► **Adolph Eichmann.**

461. ► **Oil (especially olive oil).**

462. ► **Spain and Germany.**

463. ► **"Tzedakah".**

464. ► **Damascus and Amman.**

CURRENT
EVENTS
465. ► The Israeli banking industry recently suffered serious losses because of . . . ?

WOMEN
466. ► She founded the Women's Zionist Organization, *Hadassah* . . . ?

ARTS &
CULTURE
467. ► These Jewish actors were known as the "Royal Family" of the Yiddish theater and their surname was . . . ?

PEOPLE
468. ► This noted Jewish scientist gave the first official lecture at the Hebrew University of Jerusalem . . . ?

RELIGION
469. ► What is the position of the right-wing Orthodox rabbinate on the recognition of Conservative and Reform rabbis as authentic rabbis?

HISTORY
470. ► Daniel Webster dedicated the Bunker Hill monument in Charlestown, Massachusetts, and referred to this "Christian and Jew" who made the memorial possible . . . ?

LANGUAGE
471. ► The Hebrew word *nasi* refers to?

GEOGRAPHY
472. ► Last year in Paris, what happened that was of significance to the Jewish world during the Fourth International Jewish Film Festival?

　(Answers next page.)

ANSWERS

CURRENT
EVENTS 465. ► Major devaluations of the shekel and rumors of additional devaluations that ignited sharp selling of bank stocks for the purchase of American dollars. (The banks have been accused of inflating their stock prices and concealing information from the public.)

WOMEN 466. ► Henrietta Szold.

ARTS &
CULTURE 467. ► Adler (Stella, Celia, Luther and Jacob).

PEOPLE 468. ► Albert Einstein, in 1928.

RELIGION 469. ► They do not recognize non-Orthodox rabbis as valid rabbis.

HISTORY 470. ► Judah Tuoro was the Jewish philanthropist and Amos Lawrence the Christian benefactor (in 1843).

LANGUAGE 471. ► President.

GEOGRAPHY 472. ► The theater was bombed by anti-Semitic terrorists.

CURRENT
EVENTS

473. ► How many Israeli aircraft were shot down by the Syrians during Operation Peace for Galilee?

WOMEN

474. ► After Eleazer and Phineas died, which woman ruled the holy city of Shiloh?

ARTS &
CULTURE

475. ► This Jewish actor played the role of Nazi "Colonel Klink" on the TV series *Hogan's Heroes*. . . ?

PEOPLE

476. ► This pre-state Jewish underground leader hid from the British authorities by assuming the identity of Rabbi Israel Sassover . . . ?

RELIGION

477. ► The founder of the American Conservative Jewish movement is . . . ?

HISTORY

478. ► Arthur Goldberg resigned this position when President Lyndon B. Johnson asked him to accept the appointment as U.S. Ambassador to the UN . . . ?

LANGUAGE

479. ► When does one say *l'chayim*?

GEOGRAPHY

480. ► The Maccabees were born in . . . ?

ANSWERS

473. ► None. (Over 100 Arab fighter planes were shot down. Israel lost one helicopter due to technical difficulties, not because of Syrian fire.)

WOMEN
474. ► Deborah (the great Judge).

ARTS &
CULTURE
475. ► Werner Klemperer.

PEOPLE
476. ► Menachem Begin, Commander-in-Chief of the Irgun Zvei Leumi.

RELIGION
477. ► Solomon Schechter (in 1902).

HISTORY
478. ► Associate Justice of the United States Supreme Court.

LANGUAGE
479. ► When taking a drink, usually alcohol.

GEOGRAPHY
480. ► Modiin.

CURRENT
EVENTS

481. ► Soviet diplomacy in Lebanon was recently dealt a heavy blow when this action was taken against Soviet Embassy personnel...?

WOMEN

482. ► The daughter of this early Zionist leader, who served as Tel Aviv's first mayor was a left wing radical during the 1960s and later became involved with the PLO...?

ARTS &
CULTURE

483. ► This Jewish author wrote these recent bestselling Jewish theme novels, *The Book of Rachel* and *The Lives of Rachel*...?

PEOPLE

484. ► Dr. George Habash heads the Arab terrorist organization known as PFLP. What do the initials stand for?

RELIGION

485. ► When asked to define the essence of Jewish law, he replied, "What is hateful to yourself, do not do to your neighbor"...?

HISTORY

486. ► In 1936, this Socialist leader became the first Jewish premier of France; four years later, he was a prisoner in a Nazi concentration camp...?

LANGUAGE

487. ► One who is *ferblondget* is...?

GEOGRAPHY

488. ► On the shores of Israel's Red Sea is an industry that cuts, polishes, and exports rock of this type...?

ANSWERS

CURRENT EVENTS
481. ► Four Russian diplomats stationed in Moslem West Beirut were kidnapped. (This was especially embarrassing because their main Arab ally, Syria is the power broker in Lebanon.)

WOMEN
482. ► David Rokeach. (His daughter, Livia, committed suicide in Rome in 1984.)

ARTS & CULTURE
483. ► Joel Gross.

PEOPLE
484. ► Popular Front for the Liberation of Palestine.

RELIGION
485. ► Hillel.

HISTORY
486. ► Leon Blum.

LANGUAGE
487. ► Hopelessly lost.

GEOGRAPHY
488. ► Granite.

CURRENT
EVENTS

489. ► Athletes from this country were not permitted to take part in the 12th Maccabiah Games, so some disguised themselves as new immigrants in order to participate . . . ?

WOMEN

490. ► Sara Aaronsohn was tortured to death in 1917, after being apprehended for espionage activities while assisting the British liberation of Palestine. Her execution was ordered by this country . . . ?

ARTS &
CULTURE

491. ► Harry Austryn Wolfson was the first Jewish professor to hold this distinguished chair at Harvard College . . . ?

PEOPLE

492. ► This Jewish comedian was taken off the air when he asked his "kiddy viewers" to look in their parents' handbags and send him some of "that green stuff" . . . ?

RELIGION

493. ► When are the Ten Days of Repententance?

HISTORY

494. ► Who were the misguided and cowardly *Donmeh* Jews of Turkey?

LANGUAGE

495. ► The Hebrew word *nefesh* translates to . . . ?

GEOGRAPHY

496. ► This country's Jews developed the singing of the Liturgy during the worship service to make it more closely resemble Protestant church service . . . ?

ANSWERS

CURRENT EVENTS	**489.** ▶	**South Africa.**
WOMEN	**490.** ▶	**Turkey.**
ARTS & CULTURE	**491.** ▶	**Judaic Studies.**
PEOPLE	**492.** ▶	**Soupy Sales (Milton Hines).**
RELIGION	**493.** ▶	**Between "Rosh Hashanah" and "Yom Kippur."**
HISTORY	**494.** ▶	**The Turkish Jews who became Moslems with the false Messiah, "Shabbatai Zvi." (The Turkish authorities ordered them to renounce their Jewish religion and they complied rather than face death.)**
LANGUAGE	**495.** ▶	**Soul.**
GEOGRAPHY	**496.** ▶	**Germany.**

CURRENT
EVENTS

497. ► Since it surrendered the Sinai to Egypt, Israel has had to import all of its oil. How much does this cost Israel annually (within 10% accuracy)?

WOMEN

498. ► In 1985, Amy Eilberg achieved distinction in the Conservative movement for this reason . . . ?

ARTS &
CULTURE

499. ► This carrot dish is traditionally served on *Rosh Hashanah* . . . ?

PEOPLE

500. ► This recipient of the 1976 Nobel Prize for Literature wrote a critically acclaimed personal account of his visit to Israel. Who is he and what is the title of the book?

RELIGION

501. ► This denomination within Judaism has the largest number of congregations in the United States . . . ?

HISTORY

502. ► The Jewish settlers in Palestine faced this ironic dilemma in their decision to join the British in fighting the Nazis . . . ?

LANGUAGE

503. ► The Yiddish term *Geshrei* means . . . ?

GEOGRAPHY

504. ► Until recently, this European nation did not fully recognize Judaism, so marriages had to be conducted by both religious and civil authorities to be legally accepted . . . ?

(Answers next page.)

ANSWERS

497. ► Approximately $2.5-billion (which nearly equals Israel's entire trade deficit).

WOMEN 498. ► She became their first female rabbi.

ARTS &
CULTURE 499. ► "Tzimmes".

PEOPLE 500. ► Saul Bellow, author of "To Jerusalem and Back."

RELIGION 501. ► The Orthodox.

HISTORY 502. ► The Jews of Palestine were fighting against the British for greater rights and freedoms at the same time that they agreed to help them fight the Nazis.

LANGUAGE 503. ► To yell or scream.

GEOGRAPHY 504. ► Spain.

CURRENT
EVENTS

505. ► The Soviet Union and the United States both feel that the Middle East is the best place to test these . . . ?

WOMEN

506. ► This Jewish woman on the staff of *The New Yorker* magazine is considered the dean of the New York film critics . . .

ARTS &
CULTURE

507. ► He wrote *A Jew in Love, Perfidy, The Sensualist, Child of the Century,* and other outstanding 20th century American literature . . . ?

PEOPLE

508. ► He was the first English Jew to join the House of Lords . . . ?

RELIGION

509. ► He was the founder of the Jewish Reconstructionist movement in the United States . . . ?

HISTORY

510. ► He originally built the city of Caesarea . . . ?

LANGUAGE

511. ► What is a *blech*?

GEOGRAPHY

512. ► When Blacks recently took power in this small African country, replacing the previous white minority government, nearly all of the Jewish community fled . . . ?

ANSWERS

505. ► New weapons systems.

506. ► Pauline Kael.

507. ► Ben Hecht.

508. ► Nathaniel Rothschild.

509. ► Mordecai Kaplan.

510. ► Herod the Great.

511. ► A hot plate left on the stove for the duration of the Sabbath in order to keep food warm without cooking.

512. ► Rhodesia, now called Zimbabwe.

CURRENT
EVENTS

513. ▶ On which Jewish holy site have Arabs recently built a monument accusing Israel of committing genocide?

WOMEN

514. ▶ Orthodox Jewish law requires women to observe these four *mitzvot*...?

ARTS &
CULTURE

515. ▶ This Jewish old-time comedian was born with the name Irwin Alan Kniber ...?

PEOPLE

516. ▶ Name two of the three Jewish major league baseball pitchers to throw no-hit games, one of baseball's greatest achievements...?

RELIGION

517. ▶ In which of the Torah's first five books is Moses not mentioned?

HISTORY

518. ▶ What 2 major positions did David Ben Gurion hold simultaneously in the early government of Israel?

LANGUAGE

519. ▶ One who is a *balabusta* refers to...?

GEOGRAPHY

520. ▶ The Bible mentions the Sea of the Philistines which today is know as this ocean...?

ANSWERS

513. ► On the Temple Mount in Jerusalem. (The inscriptions on the monument charge Israel with perpetrating the Sabra-Shatilla killings of 1982.)

WOMEN 514. ► 1. Keeping kosher, 2. lighting Sabbath candles, 3. baking challah, 4. following restraints on sexual contact between husband and wife.

ARTS &
CULTURE 515. ► Alan King.

PEOPLE 516. ► Sandy Koufax (four times), Ken Koltzman (twice) and Bo Belinsky (once).

RELIGION 517. ► In Genesis (the first book).

HISTORY 518. ► Defense Minister and Prime Minister.

LANGUAGE 519. ► An excellent and hospitable home-maker.

GEOGRAPHY 520. ► The Mediterranean.

CURRENT
EVENTS

521. ► According to present Jordanian law, what is the penalty for selling land to a Jew?

WOMEN

522. ► This Jewish singer-actress played Fanny Brice in the movies *Funny Girl* and *Funny Lady* . . . ?

ARTS &
CULTURE

523. ► This Jewish songwriter composed the monumental hit *Somewhere Over the Rainbow* immortalized by Judy Garland . . . ?

PEOPLE

524. ► This Jewish physicist was responsible for the discover of electromagnetic waves . . . ?

RELIGION

525. ► On Yom Kippur, according to Orthodox Jewish Law, which type of shoes are traditionally prohibited from being worn?

HISTORY

526. ► Joseph Trumpeldor helped found the Jewish Legion of the British Army—but the Legion was preceeded by another military organization, called . . . ?

LANGUAGE

527. ► What is the English translation for *Sefer Torah*?

GEOGRAPHY

528. ► Between World War I and World War II, this continent had the largest Jewish population . . . ?

ANSWERS

CURRENT
EVENTS
521. ▶ Death.

WOMEN
522. ▶ Barbra Streisand.

ARTS &
CULTURE
523. ▶ Howard Arlen.

PEOPLE
524. ▶ Heinrich R. Hertz.

RELIGION
525. ▶ Leather shoes. (When one is asking for life, it would be callous to wear leather which represents the death of an animal.)

HISTORY
526. ▶ The Zion Mule Corps.

LANGUAGE
527. ▶ Scroll of the Law.

GEOGRAPHY
528. ▶ Europe.

CURRENT
EVENTS

529. ► The more the Israeli government reduces spending in this area, the more deterrence will be compromised...?

WOMEN

530. ► One of the leading Jewish authors of children's books, she wrote *Joshua in the Promised Land, Chassidic stories for children* and *Light Another Candle*...?

ARTS &
CULTURE

531. ► This Jewish composer was the only person to award himself an Oscar at the Academy Awards ceremonies ...?

PEOPLE

532. ► Who was Bogdan Chmielnicki and what were his crimes?

RELIGION

533. ► Who was the first Jew to be circumcised at the age of eight days?

HISTORY

534. ► How did the "Black Death" plague, in 14th century Europe, affect the Jewish people?

LANGUAGE

535. ► The much overused Yiddish expression *k'nocker* means...?

GEOGRAPHY

536. ► What was the approximate number of Israelis who left their country last year to settle abroad (within 10 percent accuracy)...?

ANSWERS

529. ► The Defense Budget. (This translates as less active duty training, fewer flying hours, less research and less reserve duty.)

530. ► Miriam Chaikin.

531. ► Irving Berlin.

532. ► A Polish hero who was the Cossack leader responsible for killing hundreds of thousands of Jews (most perished from 1648 to 1649).

533. ► Isaac, son of Abraham.

534. ► They were considered the cause of it and as a result became the victims of numerous pogroms. (Jews did not suffer as badly as the rest of the population from this plague because of their kosher eating habits and their general isolation from the Christian community.)

535. ► A big shot or an old-timer.

536. ► 17,000 (according to Israel's Central Bureau of Statistics).

CURRENT
EVENTS

537. ► Israel holds the world record for having the highest percentage of its citizens employed by the government. Within 5%, what is this percentage?

WOMEN

538. ► This well-known Jewish French stage actress was an illegitmate child, had a wooden leg, and was fond of sleeping in a coffin . . . ?

ARTS &
CULTURE

539. ► This Jewish actor played Harry Houdini in the 1953 movie *Houdini* . . . ?

PEOPLE

540. ► This Israeli statesman was born with the name Aubrey Solomon, but is better known by this name . . . ?

RELIGION

541. ► This Book of the Bible is a series of farewell speeches by Moses, and it ends with a description of his death . . . ?

HISTORY

542. ► What was the significant difference between the resettlement movement in Palestine, in the early 1900s, and the movement during World War II known as *Aliyah Bet*?

LANGUAGE

543. ► The Hebrew word *Seder* means . . . ?

GEOGRAPHY

544. ► This European country was so fierce in its persecution of Jews that in 1893 the Jewish population formed an organization for its own self-defense . . . ?

(Answers next page.)

ANSWERS

CURRENT EVENTS 537. ► Approximately 35%.

WOMEN 538. ► Sarah Bernhardt.

ARTS & CULTURE 539. ► Tony Curtis (who was born Bernard Schwartz, played Harry Houdini— who was born Eric Weiss).

PEOPLE 540. ► Abba Eban.

RELIGION 541. ► Deuteronomy.

HISTORY 542. ► The early movement was legal and sanctioned by Turkey and Britain. "Aliyah Bet" was illegal and involved the smuggling of Holocaust survivors out of Europe.

LANGUAGE 543. ► Order of service.

GEOGRAPHY 544. ► Germany.

CURRENT
EVENTS
545. ► Presently, the largest arms supplier to Saudi Arabia is...?

WOMEN
546. ► This Swiss-born Jewish female became Vermont's first woman governor...?

ARTS &
CULTURE
547. ► This old-time Jewish comedian and T.V. personality was born Joseph Abraham Gottlieb, but he used the stage name...?

PEOPLE
548. ► Jewish entrepreneur Julius Rosenwald, built this company into America's largest retailer and mail order business ...?

RELIGION
549. ► In Israel, *suvganiot*, or doughnuts filled with jam, are associated with which holiday?

HISTORY
550. ► Although England is a democratic nation, what position in the British Empire is strictly off limits to Jews?

LANGUAGE
551. ► What is *Chanukah gelt* and who is it given to?

GEOGRAPHY
552. ► The Gulf of Eilat is the meeting place of the land of which 3 Middle East nations?

ANSWERS

CURRENT EVENTS
545. ► The United States of America.

WOMEN
546. ► Madeline Kunin (in 1985).

ARTS & CULTURE
547. ► Joey Bishop.

PEOPLE
548. ► Sears Roebuck.

RELIGION
549. ► Chanukah (because they are fried in oil).

HISTORY
550. ► The position of Monarch. (There has been no serious Jewish protest over this restriction!)

LANGUAGE
551. ► Small gifts of money given to children as Chanukah presents.

GEOGRAPHY
552. ► Israel, Jordan and Saudi Arabia.

CURRENT
EVENTS

553. ► To which countries did the PLO transfer its headquarters when it was expelled from Beirut in 1982?

WOMEN

554. ► This Biblical matriach was not laid to rest with the other three...?

ARTS &
CULTURE

555. ► This dish, served at the Passover Seder, symbolizes the mortar used by Jewish slaves in Egypt...?

PEOPLE

556. ► What was Israeli Prime Minister Shimon Peres originally named at birth?

RELIGION

557. ► What did Jesus, Mohammed and Joseph Smith have in common?

HISTORY

558. ► This racist and anti-Semitic organization was originally financed by Judah Benjamin, a Jewish leader of the Confederacy, to fight disorderly elements after the Civil War...?

LANGUAGE

559. ► The Yiddish term *mishmosh* means...?

GEOGRAPHY

560. ► Name one of the two minerals besides salt which are extracted in large quantities from the waters of the Dead Sea...?

ANSWERS

CURRENT EVENTS   553. ► First Tunisia and most recently Jordan.

WOMEN   554. ► Rachel. (She was buried in a tomb on the road to Bethlehem.)

ARTS & CULTURE   555. ► "Charoses."

PEOPLE   556. ► Shimon Persky.

RELIGION   557. ► They all claimed to have spoken to God, and then went on to establish major world religions. (Christianity, Islam, Mormonism.)

HISTORY   558. ► The Ku Klux Klan (originally it was not a dangerous and racist organization).

LANGUAGE   559. ► Hodgepodge.

GEOGRAPHY   560. ► Potash and bromine.

CURRENT
EVENTS

561. ► What do Italy's *Red Brigades*, Argentina's *Montoneros* and the *Eritrean Liberation Front* all have in common?

WOMEN

562. ► Brenda Patimkim is the heroine of this 1959 Philip Roth bestseller...?

ARTS &
CULTURE

563. ► This Israeli writer won the 1966 Nobel Prize for Literature...?

PEOPLE

564. ► This Israeli mayor once publicly compared Menachem Begin to Idi Amin...?

RELIGION

565. ► England's Reform Jewish Movement is called...?

HISTORY

566. ► This rightwing Zionist youth movement played a key role in the Warsaw Ghetto uprising against the Nazis...?

LANGUAGE

567. ► The Hebrew word *brit* means...?

GEOGRAPHY

568. ► The Dead Sea Scrolls and other ancient manuscripts are displayed in this Israeli institution...?

ANSWERS

CURRENT EVENTS	561. ►	They are all linked to the PLO terror network.
WOMEN	562. ►	"Goodbye Columbus".
ARTS & CULTURE	563. ►	S.Y. Agnon.
PEOPLE	564. ►	Mayor Teddy Kollek of Jerusalem.
RELIGION	565. ►	The Liberal Jewish Union.
HISTORY	566. ►	"Betar".
LANGUAGE	567. ►	Covenant.
GEOGRAPHY	568. ►	The Shrine of the Book which is part of the Israel Museum in Jerusalem.

CURRENT
EVENTS
   569. ► This 1984 American Presidential candidate surprisingly criticized Israel's rescue of Ethiopian Jews...?

WOMEN
   570. ► This Israeli Prime Minister was raised in Milwaukee, Wisconsin...?

ARTS &
CULTURE
   571. ► This Jewish film maker directed *All the President's Men* and *Sophie's Choice* ...?

PEOPLE
   572. ► The Reagan administration had reportedly asked these two prominent Jewish figures, both long associated with the Holocaust, to accompany the President to the Bitburg Cemetery. One writes about it, the other brings the perpetrators to justice; both declined this invitation...?

RELIGION
   573. ► Why is it impossible to seriously believe in both Judaism *and* Communism simultaneously?

HISTORY
   574. ► How did Adolph Hitler die?

LANGUAGE
   575. ► The Yiddish word *nosh* refers to...?

GEOGRAPHY
   576. ► This ancient fortress is located in the northern Galilee, a few miles west of the upper Jordan river...?

ANSWERS

CURRENT
EVENTS

577. ► In what city has the Egyptian Ambassador to Israel been stationed from 1982 through 1985?

WOMEN

578. ► This English novelist, born Mary Anne Evans, is the author of *Daniel Deronda* which demonstrates her sympathy for the Jewish people through its Zionist motif...?

ARTS &
CULTURE

579. ► This controversial Jewish comedian died of a drug overdose in 1966...?

PEOPLE

580. ► When Menachem Begin was elected Prime Minister in 1977, he appointed this former Labor Party leader as his foreign minister...?

RELIGION

581. ► Reform Judaism introduced this ceremony for the young people who attended its religious schools...?

HISTORY

582. ► Name the two Jews most responsible for creating the *Jewish Legion* which fought in World War I...?

LANGUAGE

583. ► The common Hebrew word *ben* translates to...?

GEOGRAPHY

584. ► This Israeli port is north of Saudi Arabia's shore...?

ANSWERS

577. ► **Cairo. He was recalled from Israel in 1982, and as of late 1985, he has not been sent back.**

578. ► **George Eliot. (She chose a male name as her pseudonym.)**

579. ► **Lenny Bruce.**

580. ► **Moshe Dayan.**

581. ► **The Confirmation Ceremony. (This occurs on Shavuos).**

582. ► **Joseph Trumpeldor and Ze'ev Jabotinsky.**

583. ► **Son of.**

584. ► **Eilat.**

CURRENT EVENTS

585. ▶ What was the major controversy over the joint U.S.-Arab launching of the Arabsat communications satellite?

WOMEN

586. ▶ Who did the Persian King Ahasuerus divorce before marrying Esther?

ARTS & CULTURE

587. ▶ This Jewish scientist was the only person to ever win two Nobel Prizes...?

PEOPLE

588. ▶ This deceased American black leader has a forest named after him in northern Israel...?

RELIGION

589. ▶ This daily Prayer Book is used in Reform Synagogues...?

HISTORY

590. ▶ He was the only criminal ever to receive capital punishment in the modern State of Israel...?

LANGUAGE

591. ▶ The Yiddish term *noodge* refers to...?

GEOGRAPHY

592. ▶ The Pillars of Solomon are located at ...?

ANSWERS

585. ▶ **The consortium of Arab States involved included the PLO, implying an in-
formal recognition by the U.S. (The
State Department claims that this project involved an agreement between the
U.S. and an international organization.
It is interesting to note that during the
flight, the saudi prince astronaut displayed a PLO flag.)**

WOMEN **586.** ▶ **Vashti.**

ARTS &
CULTURE **587.** ▶ **Dr. Linus Pauling (Chemistry in 1954
and the Peace Prize in 1962).**

PEOPLE **588.** ▶ **Martin Luther King, Jr.**

RELIGION **589.** ▶ **The Union Prayer Book.**

HISTORY **590.** ▶ **Adolf Eichmann, the Nazi murderer.**

LANGUAGE **591.** ▶ **An annoying person.**

GEOGRAPHY **592.** ▶ **The entrance to the Timna copper
mines in Israel's Negev desert.**

CURRENT
EVENTS

593. ► These are the only two South American countries that have embassies in Jerusalem rather than Tel Aviv . . . ?

WOMEN

594. ► This famous 1946 conference marked a turning point for women within Judaism. Reform rabbis stated: "It is our sacred duty to declare with all emphasis the complete religious equality of women" . . . ?

ARTS &
CULTURE

595. ► This anti-Semitic European dictator was *Time Magazine's* "Man of the Year" in 1937 . . . ?

PEOPLE

596. ► This former mayor of a major southern U.S. city was fired from his new post in the Carter Administration when he met with a PLO official . . . ?

RELIGION

597. ► What was the attitude of Isaac Mayer Wise and his followers towards the Zionist movement?

HISTORY

598. ► The name of the Chief of the Israeli Mossad is never made public. He or she is referred to as . . . ?

LANGUAGE

599. ► A *Zaftig* woman refers to one who is . . . ?

GEOGRAPHY

600. ► What body of water is found southwest of the Sinai?

ANSWERS

CURRENT
EVENTS
601. ► This U.S. Christian group operates an East Jerusalem legal aid center for PLO suspects . . . ?

WOMEN
602. ► She was the first woman to become a minister in the government of Menachem Begin . . . ?

ARTS &
CULTURE
603. ► These two Jewish comedian-actors won Tony Awards for their roles in the 1963 and 1972 productions of *A Funny Thing Happened On the Way to the Forum* . . . ?

PEOPLE
604. ► He was an outstanding personality in the U.S. labor movement and in 1932 became president of the International Ladies Garment Workers' Union? . . .

RELIGION
605. ► These characteristics identify an animal that is kosher . . . ?

HISTORY
606. ► The British controlled Palestine during these years . . . ?

LANGUAGE
607. ► What Ladino word meaning "barbarian" was commonly used by *Sephardim* when they referred to *Ashkenazim*?

GEOGRAPHY
608. ► This Egyptian city, located on the Mediterranean Sea, is known as the *Capital of the Sinai* . . . ?

ANSWERS

601. ▶ **The American Friends Service Committee of the Quakers.**

602. ▶ **Sara Doron, of the Liberal Party (appointed Minister Without Portfolio in 1983).**

603. ▶ **Zero Mostel and Phil Silvers.**

604. ▶ **David Dubinsky.**

605. ▶ **It must chew its cud and have split hooves.**

606. ▶ **1917 to 1948.**

607. ▶ **"Todesta."**

608. ▶ **El'Arish.**

609. ► Israel's recently-enacted Anti-Mission-
ary Law does not prohibit missioniz-
ing. What does it prohibit?

WOMEN **610.** ► In 1974, the Reconstructionist Rabbinical College did what the Reform
rabbinical seminary had done in 1972
. . . ?

ARTS &
CULTURE **611.** ► *Commentary*, the prestigious Jewish
magazine, is published by this Jewish
organization . . . ?

PEOPLE **612.** ► This Israeli was hanged in Damascus
Square in May 1965, for spying and
was known by the alias, Kamil Amin
Taqbes. He is fondly remembered as
"Our Man in Damascus" . . . ?

RELIGION **613.** ► Which modern Christian group is influenced by the idea of a Jewish God? .

HISTORY **614.** ► About how many Jews of Polish origin
perished in the Holocaust . . . ?

LANGUAGE **615.** ► The Hebrew religious term *muktzeh*,
refers to . . . ?

GEOGRAPHY **616.** ► The South Lebanon Army captured 21
prisoners of the U.N. Interim Force in
Lebanon and held them for eight days.
The detainees came from this nation
. . . ?

ANSWERS

CURRENT EVENTS **609.** ▶ **It prohibits missionaries from bribing potential converts, but does not restrict any other proselytizing activities.**

WOMEN **610.** ▶ **It ordained its first woman as a rabbi.**

ARTS & CULTURE **611.** ▶ **The American Jewish Committee.**

PEOPLE **612.** ▶ **Eli Cohen.**

RELIGION **613.** ▶ **The Unitarians.**

HISTORY **614.** ▶ **Three million.**

LANGUAGE **615.** ▶ **Items that should not be touched on the Sabbath or on certain holidays (i.e. money, machines, work tools).**

GEOGRAPHY **616.** ▶ **Finland.**

CURRENT
EVENTS   **617.** ► The West Bank Arab town of Arraheh was the center of this hoax on the Israeli government in 1983...?

WOMEN   **618.** ► This well-known gentile actress publicly denounced her Jewish critics as "a small bunch of Zionist hooligans"...?

ARTS &
CULTURE   **619.** ► This Jewish movie mogul was known to sit in the front of movie theaters with his back to the screen, in order to watch the audience's reactions...?

PEOPLE   **620.** ► He was the King of England at the time of the Balfour Declaration, which was issued on November 29, 1917...?

RELIGION   **621.** ► The Ashkenazim call this the *Aron ha-Kodesh*, the Sephardim call it *Hei Khal*—the place in the synagogue where the Torah scrolls are kept...?

HISTORY   **622.** ► When did Israel and Egypt fight the "War of Attrition"?

LANGUAGE   **623.** ► In what language is the traditional Jewish wedding contract, the *Ketubah*, written?

GEOGRAPHY   **624.** ► Where is the Gulf of Clysma?

ANSWERS

617. ► Hundreds of Arab schoolgirls pretended to be ill and claimed that the Israelis had "poisoned" them.

618. ► Vanessa Redgrave.

619. ► Samuel Goldwyn.

620. ► King George V.

621. ► The Ark.

622. ► 1969-1970. (While terrorist activity occurred after the Six-Day War, all out fighting erupted in 1969 and continued until the U.S.-mediated cease fire in 1970.)

623. ► Aramaic.

624. ► In the Suez Canal.

CURRENT
EVENTS

625. ► When Nazi war criminal Soobzokov was killed in a recent New Jersey bomb blast, this Jewish group was suspected of planting the bomb . . . ?

WOMEN

626. ► This book of the Bible, named after a woman, never mentions the name of God . . . ?

ARTS &
CULTURE

627. ► The box-office classic, *Samson and Delilah*, was adapted from a book authored by this controversial Zionist leader . . . ?

PEOPLE

628. ► This young Jewish lawyer gained fame as Committee Council at the McCarthy hearings of the early 1950's . . . ?

RELIGION

629. ► How did two Jewish collaborators help Mohammed?

HISTORY

630. ► Abba Eban, in describing Israel's pre-1967 borders, compared them to a concentration camp, calling them . . . ?

LANGUAGE

631. ► What are the literal and figurative meanings of the Yiddish word *shmaltz*?

GEOGRAPHY

632. ► The Levantine Jews come from this area . . . ?

(Answers next page.)

ANSWERS

<table>
<tr><td>CURRENT
EVENTS</td><td>625. ►</td><td>The Jewish Defense League. (JDL national director Fern Rosenblatt said that the JDL "applauded" the assasination.)</td></tr>
<tr><td>WOMEN</td><td>626. ►</td><td>The Book of Esther.</td></tr>
<tr><td>ARTS &
CULTURE</td><td>627. ►</td><td>Vladimir Ze'ev Jabotinsky, author of "Prelude to Delilah".</td></tr>
<tr><td>PEOPLE</td><td>628. ►</td><td>Roy Cohn.</td></tr>
<tr><td>RELIGION</td><td>629. ►</td><td>They assisted him in editing the Koran.</td></tr>
<tr><td>HISTORY</td><td>630. ►</td><td>"Auschwitz Lines"—because they could lead to the worst tragedy since Auschwitz: the destruction of Israel.</td></tr>
<tr><td>LANGUAGE</td><td>631. ►</td><td>Literal: chicken fat. Figurative: extreme sentimentality.</td></tr>
<tr><td>GEOGRAPHY</td><td>632. ►</td><td>Asia Minor.</td></tr>
</table>

CURRENT
EVENTS

633. ► Last year, a U.S. official surrendered his citizenship and returned to his native Germany after the Justice Department revealed he had persecuted slave laborers in a Nazi V-2 factory during WW II. He worked in this U.S. governmental agency...?

WOMEN

634. ► In the early years of the 20th Century, this Jewish American, Sophie Irene Simon Loeb, was a world-renowned activist and the prime mover for new legislation in this neglected area...?

ARTS &
CULTURE

635. ► This Jewish comedian played the role of Rufus T. Firefly in his beloved movies ...?

PEOPLE

636. ► This 1960's radical, a member of the Chicago Seven, is now an active supporter of the PLO...?

RELIGION

637. ► What is *Shmura Matzah*?

HISTORY

638. ► In 1969, this Israeli organization allegedly stole the blueprints for the Mirage III fighter jet from Switzerland ...?

LANGUAGE

639. ► This language is spoken by most of the Christian citizens of Israel...?

GEOGRAPHY

640. ► What Jewish Holy city has 110,000 Moslem and 14,000 Christian inhabitants?

ANSWERS

633. ▶ NASA.

634. ▶ Laws protecting the rights of children.

635. ▶ Groucho Marx.

636. ▶ David Dellinger.

637. ▶ Literally, guarded matzah. It is the matzah eaten on Passover by the most pious Jews. (Every stage of the production process is carefully monitored.)

638. ▶ The "Mossad." (The Israeli CIA.)

639. ▶ Arabic.

640. ▶ Jerusalem.

CURRENT
EVENTS   641. ► Who was the *Herut* Party's first candidate for Prime Minister of Israel . . . ?

WOMEN   642. ► These Jewish twin sisters with American-sounding adopted names have competing newspaper columns. . . ?

ARTS &
CULTURE   643. ► David Ricardo was a famous Jewish 19th century theoretician known as the father of which branch of the social sciences. . . ?

PEOPLE   644. ► He was the Secretary-General of the United Nations during the 1967 Six-Day-War. . . ?

RELIGION   645. ► During this holiday we say, "And for all of them, O God of forgiveness, forgive us". . . ?

HISTORY   646. ► On the day that Israel declared its independence, Chaim Weizmann and Abba Eban were not in Israel. They were both in. . . ?

LANGUAGE   647. ► The frequently-used Yiddish term to describe someone who is crazy or mad is . . . ?

GEOGRAPHY   648. ► This river is the longest in Israel. . . ?

ANSWERS

<table>
<tr><td>CURRENT EVENTS</td><td>641.</td><td>► Menachem Begin (in 1977).</td></tr>
<tr><td>WOMEN</td><td>642.</td><td>► Ann Landers (Esther Friedman) and Abigail Van Buren (Pauline Friedman).</td></tr>
<tr><td>ARTS & CULTURE</td><td>643.</td><td>► Economics.</td></tr>
<tr><td>PEOPLE</td><td>644.</td><td>► U Thant.</td></tr>
<tr><td>RELIGION</td><td>645.</td><td>► Yom Kippur.</td></tr>
<tr><td>HISTORY</td><td>646.</td><td>► New York City as Israel's delegates to the United Nations. (Israel was not formally admitted to the U.N. for another year.)</td></tr>
<tr><td>LANGUAGE</td><td>647.</td><td>► "Meshuggeh" or Meshuggehneh."</td></tr>
<tr><td>GEOGRAPHY</td><td>648.</td><td>► The Jordan.</td></tr>
</table>

CURRENT
EVENTS

649. ► What are the negative intentions of the recently formed non-Jewish coalition of Ukranian, Estonian, Latvian and Lithuanian organizations?

WOMEN

650. ► This Polish-born Jewish woman built an empire in the American cosmetics business...?

ARTS &
CULTURE

651. ► This non-Jewish 19th century American poet wrote *The Jewish Cemetery at Newport*...?

PEOPLE

652. ► This Jewish lawyer was appointed by President Franklin D. Roosevelt to the United States Supreme Court...?

RELIGION

653. ► Under these circumstances, some Jews sit *shiva* even though no one has died ...?

HISTORY

654. ► On March 16, 1190, there was another occurence in Jewish history, besides Masada, when besieged Jews chose suicide rather than submit to capture and ignoble death. Where did this happen?

LANGUAGE

655. ► On February 24, 1949, Israel and this Arab nation signed an agreement following the War of Independence...?

GEOGRAPHY

656. ► The Nazis planned a major "Museum of the Extinct Race" in this Eastern European city...?

ANSWERS

CURRENT
EVENTS

649. ► To hinder the work of the U.S. Justice Department's Nazi-hunting Office of Special Investigations. (Similar moves are also taking place in Canada where they are succeeding in slowing down or dissuading investigations.)

WOMEN

650. ► Helena Rubinstein.

ARTS &
CULTURE

651. ► Henry Wadsworth Longfellow.

PEOPLE

652. ► Felix Frankfurter.

RELIGION

653. ► When a child intermarries or converts from the Jewish religion.

HISTORY

654. ► In York, England more than 500 Jews chose suicide in the castle where they had sought protection rather than face certain death at the hands of the anti-Semitic murderous mob outside. (They started a fire inside the castle and all perished.)

LANGUAGE

655. ► Egypt (signed in Rhodes).

GEOGRAPHY

656. ► Prague.

164

CURRENT
EVENTS

657. ► In 1983, anti-Semites opened fire on several students at this New York City Jewish institution . . . ?

WOMEN

658. ► What was *The Heartbreak Kid's* self-hating Jewish theme?

ARTS &
CULTURE

659. ► This Jewish tough-guy actor played the role of Popeye Doyle, in a popular 1970 action movie . . . ?

PEOPLE

660. ► He was the Israeli Chief-of-Staff during the Entebbe rescue mission . . . ?

RELIGION

661. ► In 1984, these religious authorities issued a joint statment asserting that "Reform Jews are Jews, just like us" . . . ?

HISTORY

662. ► The *Nili* underground, organized in Palestine during World War I, was a . . . ?

LANGUAGE

663. ► The Hebrew word *Maccabee* translates into . . . ?

GEOGRAPHY

664. ► What did Nelson Glueck discover at Ezion Gever . . . ?

ANSWERS

657. ▶ **Yeshiva University.**

658. ▶ **Its negative portrayal of Jewish women while it glamorized non-Jewish women.**

659. ▶ **Gene Hackman (in "The French Connection").**

660. ▶ **General Mordechai ("Motta") Gur.**

661. ▶ **Israel's two chief rabbis.**

662. ▶ **Jewish underground intelligence group that supplied the British with information in their fight against the Turks.**

663. ▶ **Hammer.**

664. ▶ **King Solomon's Mines.**

CURRENT EVENTS   **665.** ► He was the first major Arab leader to visit the State of Israel...?

WOMEN   **666.** ► She devoted her life to Jewish communal and intellectual activity, working for the Jewish Publication Society and founding a major American women's organization...?

ARTS & CULTURE   **667.** ► In this 1970s movie, Gene Wilder played an Orthodox Jew attempting, among other things, to speak Yiddish to Amish Pennsylvania Dutch farmers wearing long black coats...?

PEOPLE   **668.** ► Spain's Francisco Franco felt this way about diplomatic relations with Israel...?

RELIGION   **669.** ► The Conservative Movement was originally called...?

HISTORY   **670.** ► At what point in Jewish history did large numbers of Jews migrate to Holland?

LANGUAGE   **671.** ► The Yiddish and Hebrew term *mashumed* refers to one who has...?

GEOGRAPHY   **672.** ► The well-known Hassidic rabbi, Levi Yitzhak, was associated with this town...?

ANSWERS

CURRENT
EVENTS   665. ► **Anwar Sadat.**

WOMEN   666. ► **Henrietta Szold.**

ARTS &
CULTURE   667. ► **"The Frisco Kid."**

PEOPLE   668. ► **Adamant in his insistence that no such ties be established.**

RELIGION   669. ► **Historical Judaism.**

HISTORY   670. ► **After they were expelled from Spain.**

LANGUAGE   671. ► **Converted to Christianity ("a destroyed one").**

GEOGRAPHY   672. ► **Berdichev. (A book abut him has been written called Levi Yitzhak of Berdichev, by Samuel H. Dressner.)**

CURRENT
EVENTS

673. ► He was the President of Sudan at the time of the secret airlift of Jewish refugees to Israel...?

WOMEN

674. ► Published in 1955, it was the first major American literary work to portray the struggle of a Jewish female passing from girlhood to womanhood...?

ARTS &
CULTURE

675. ► The general Jewish view on organ transplants is...?

PEOPLE

676. ► He was the second prime minister of the State of Israel...?

RELIGION

677. ► This anti-Semitic Pope burned all copies of the Talmud in Paris and Rome in the 13th century...?

HISTORY

678. ► What was the crime that French army officer Wilfred Dreyfus was charged with?

LANGUAGE

679. ► In Yiddish, when a social match is made between two people it is known as a...?

GEOGRAPHY

680. ► What two nations emerged from the dismantling of the Turkish-Ottoman Empire, first as British Mandates in 1921, and later as independent nations, in 1932 and 1946?

(Answers next page.)

ANSWERS

673. ► Gaafar Nimeiry.

674. ► "Marjorie Morningstar," by Herman Wouk.

675. ► Organ transplants are allowed because saving a human life outweighs all other considerations.

676. ► Moshe Sharrett.

677. ► Pope Gregory IX.

678. ► Transferring secret French papers to the Germans. (He spent time in prison until the charges were dropped because it became clear that documents used as evidence against him were forged.)

679. ► "Shiddach."

680. ► Iraq (in 1932) and Transjordan (in 1946).

CURRENT
EVENTS

681. ► The Anti-Defamation League, B'nai B'rith International and the American Jewish Committee all hailed the recent Supreme Court decision that did what in Alabama...?

WOMEN

682. ► The *Torah* describes this dynamic woman as a great Israelite ruler who led her followers in battle...?

ARTS &
CULTURE

683. ► He was the Jewish actor who played a cowboy on a successful TV series. Who was the other Jewish cowboy in his family on this show?

PEOPLE

684. ► The first century Romans called him "King of the Jews"...?

RELIGION

685. ► The spiritual leaders of the Ethiopian Jewish community are known as...?

HISTORY

686. ► Anwar Sadat visited Israel in this year ...?

LANGUAGE

687. ► In Yiddish, one who is *ongeblassen* is ...?

GEOGRAPHY

688. ► Before 1948, the State of Israel was called...?

ANSWERS

681. ▶ Struck down an Alabama law that authorized one minute of silent prayer daily in public schools.

682. ▶ Deborah.

683. ▶ Lorne Greene and Michael Landon, in "Bonanza." (Landon is half Jewish.)

684. ▶ Jesus (in Hebrew, Yehoshua).

685. ▶ Kess (the equivalent of rabbis—known as Jewish High Priests).

686. ▶ 1977.

687. ▶ Conceited or arrogant.

688. ▶ Palestine.

CURRENT
EVENTS

689. ► What is the reason for the sudden resurgence of interest by Israeli citizens to join a kibbutz?

WOMEN

690. ► This humorous old-time Jewish actress-comic refers to her husband as "Fang" . . .?

ARTS &
CULTURE

691. ► The Bezale School of Arts and Crafts is located in this world capital . . .?

PEOPLE

692. ► During the Jewish rebellion in Jerusalem, this young Jew became the first to be hanged by the British . . .?

RELIGION

693. ► The very first sentence of the Bible is . . .?

HISTORY

694. ► This world event precipitated the collapse of the Ottoman-Turkish empire . . .?

LANGUAGE

695. ► The Yiddish term to describe all of one's relatives is . . .?

GEOGRAPHY

696. ► In 1935, these three nations had the largest Jewish populations in the world . . .?

(Answers next page.)

ANSWERS

CURRENT EVENTS **689.** ► **The fear of unemployment and economic hardships to come.**

WOMEN **690.** ► **Phyllis Diller.**

ARTS & CULTURE **691.** ► **Jerusalem.**

PEOPLE **692.** ► **Shlomo Ben-Yosef.**

RELIGION **693.** ► **"In the beginning God created the heaven and the earth.".**

HISTORY **694.** ► **World War I.**

LANGUAGE **695.** ► **"Mishpocheh."**

GEOGRAPHY **696.** ► **The United States, the Soviet Union and Poland.**

CURRENT
EVENTS

697. ► Moderate Arab leaders recognize that Israel is not their primary enemy; rather the most serious threat comes from this person. . . ?

WOMEN

698. ► This Jewish Playboy Bunny-model-singer had a long, publicized affair with Hugh Hefner. . . ?

ARTS &
CULTURE

699. ► This American civil-rights leader is the Chairman of the Black Americans to Support Israel Committee. . . ?

PEOPLE

700. ► He was the first Jew to hold a Cabinet post in the U.S. Government. . . ?

RELIGION

701. ► The largest Orthodox Jewish religious organization in the United States is. . . ?

HISTORY

702. ► When Jews first arrived in the New Word, this politician requested that the board of directors of the West India Company "Require them in a friendly way to depart. . . that the deceitful race . . . be not allowed further to infect and trouble their new colony. . . ?

LANGUAGE

703. ► Israel's equivalent of the Central Intelligence Agency is. . . ?

GEOGRAPHY

704. ► This city was the capital of ancient Israel when the Kingdom was divided . . . ?

ANSWERS

697. ► Ayatollah Khomeni.

698. ► Barbi Benton (born Barbara Klein).

699. ► The Reverend Bayard Rustin.

700. ► Oscar S. Straus, Secretary of Commerce and Labor for President Theodore Roosevelt.

701. ► The Union of Orthodox Jewish Congregations of America.

702. ► Governor Peter Stuyvesant. (A counter petition raised by Portuguese Jews who were principal stockholders in the company persuaded the directors to refuse the request.)

703. ► The "Mossad". (It handles foreign intelligence operations.)

704. ► Shechem.

CURRENT
EVENTS

705. ► This 1984 American Presidential candidate said, "If I was an Israeli, I would join Peace Now"....?

WOMEN

706. ► Most of this Jewish comedienne's jokes are about herself. She changed her name from Molinsky and has a husband named Edgar...?

ARTS &
CULTURE

707. ► A former Revisionist leader, he wrote the two volume biography of Vladimir Ze'ev Jabotinsky, entitled *Rebel and Statesman* and *Fighter and Prophet* ...?

PEOPLE

708. ► The former Mayor of Omaha, Nebraska, he was the first Jew to represent his state in the U.S. Senate...?

RELIGION

709. ► When, if ever, did Moses enter the Promised Land?

HISTORY

710. ► The Jewish people were forced to wear an identifying badge for the first time by...?

LANGUAGE

711. ► Territorialists and Zionists differed regarding this aspect of the eventual geographic location of the Jewish homeland...?

GEOGRAPHY

712. ► The only Communist nation which has formal diplomatic relations with the State of Israel is...?

ANSWERS

CURRENT
EVENTS   705. ► Jesse Jackson.

WOMEN   706. ► Joan Rivers (born Joan Molinsky).

ARTS &
CULTURE   707. ► Joseph B. Schectman.

PEOPLE   708. ► Senator Edward Zorinsky.

RELIGION   709. ► Never — he was in sight of it when he died.

HISTORY   710. ► Caliph Omar II (in the 9th Century).

LANGUAGE   711. ► Territorialists would accept any practical area that was available, while Zionists would only accept Palestine as a legitimate homeland for the Jewish People.

GEOGRAPHY   712. ► Rumania.

CURRENT
EVENTS
713. ► According to the American Jewish Committee's report on the Vatican, the reason that the Vatican withholds formal diplomatic recognition of Israel is that it fears . . . ?

WOMEN
714. ► This well-known Jewish singer was born with the family name Ethel Zimmerman . . . ?

ARTS &
CULTURE
715. ► This is the language spoken by most Jews in the world today . . . ?

PEOPLE
716. ► This Israeli leader is planning to write a book which will be a personal saga about the Holocaust and Israel's birth. It is provisionally titled, *The Generation of Destruction and Redemption* . . . ?

RELIGION
717. ► This Jewish holiday is often considered as the basis for the first ancient Jewish contribution to the drama . . . ?

HISTORY
718. ► In 1979 *Ashdod* became the first Israeli ship to do what?

LANGUAGE
719. ► The uncomplimentary Yiddish term *Nishtgootnick* refers to . . . ?

WOMEN
720. ► The approximate world Jewish population is (within 10 percent accuracy) . . . ?

(Answers next page.)

ANSWERS

CURRENT EVENTS 713. ► With full recognition, Arab-Moslem fanatics in the Mideast and Africa will launch a wave of reprisal attacks against millions of Christians in predominantly Islamic countries.

WOMEN 714. ► Ethel Merman.

ARTS & CULTURE 715. ► English.

PEOPLE 716. ► Former Prime Minister Menachem Begin.

RELIGION 717. ► The Purim celebration and its dramatization of the story of Haman and Esther.

HISTORY 718. ► Go through the Suez Canal after the 1979 Israeli-Egyptian Peace Treaty.

LANGUAGE 719. ► A good-for-nothing.

GEOGRAPHY 720. ► 14.5 million people. (According to the World Zionist Handbook.)

Trivia Judaica.

CURRENT EVENTS **721.** ▶ Iraq's biggest financ͏͏
war with Israel is . . .

WOMEN **722.** ▶ Why would an insta͏
highly unlikely?

ARTS & CULTURE **723.** ▶ This Polish Jewish authoɪ wrote the books *Being There* and *The Painted Bird* . . . ?

PEOPLE **724.** ▶ In 1958, this Israeli Foreign Minister said, "Is the world really asking too much if it demands of this vast Arab empire that it live in peace and harmony with a little state, established in the cradle of its birth . . . within the narrowest territory in which its natural purposes can ever be fulfilled . . ."?

RELIGION **725.** ▶ New York's Jewish Theological Seminary is affiliated with this denomination within Judaism . . . ?

HISTORY **726.** ▶ In 1891, the Jews of Corfu, Greece, were aggrieved by this spurious accusation . . . ?

LANGUAGE **727.** ▶ Who are *yordim*?

GEOGRAPHY **728.** ▶ In what body of water are the *Abu Rudez* oil fields?

(Answers next page.)

ANSWERS

721. ► Saudi Arabia.

722. ► By definition it is supposed to stew all night because of the prohibition against cooking on the Sabbath. (Instant versions would be ridiculed.)

723. ► Jerzy Kozinski.

724. ► Abba Eban.

725. ► Conservative.

726. ► They were accused of blood libel (using the blood of Christian children to make matzoh).

727. ► Israelis who emigrate permanently. (The word literally means "one who has descended" and may be used pejoratively.)

728. ► The Gulf of Suez.

CURRENT
EVENTS   **729.** ► The three major Israeli political parties which comprise the *Likud* bloc are . . . ?

WOMEN   **730.** ► This Jewish actress won an Academy Award for Best Supporting Actress in *The Diary of Anne Frank.* Her real last name is Schrift . . . ?

ARTS &
CULTURE   **731.** ► What is the name of the Zionist organization commonly referred to by the initials NAAM . . . ?

PEOPLE   **732.** ► He is Israel's greatest tennis player . . . ?

RELIGION   **733.** ► A famous Biblical proverb suggests this is the best way to answer a fool . . . ?

HISTORY   **734.** ► During the War of Independence, Egypt recalled troops threatening Jerusalem and redeployed them in preparation for an Israeli offensive in the Negev. This happened because reconnaissance planes reported a major build-up of Israeli forces. Israeli forces were actually listening to . . . ?

LANGUAGE   **735.** ► The uncomplimentary Yiddish term *nachshlepper* describes one who . . . ?

GEOGRAPHY   **736.** ► This Jewish food item is named after the Russian City of Bialystock . . . ?

ANSWERS

729. ► The "Herut" Party, the Liberal Party and the "La'am" Party (recently "La'am" merged with "Herut").

WOMEN 730. ► Shelley Winters (born Shirley Schrift).

ARTS & CULTURE 731. ► North American Aliyah Movement.

PEOPLE 732. ► Shlomo Glickstein.

RELIGION 733. ► "According to his own folly."

HISTORY 734. ► A Leonard Bernstein open air concert for 4,000 IDF soldiers—to celebrate the liberation of Beersheba.

LANGUAGE 735. ► Follows after or hangs onto.

GEOGRAPHY 736 ► A Bialy.

CURRENT
EVENTS

737. ► Jews comprise what percent of the population of the United States?

WOMEN

738. ► This Jewish actress is the daughter of a noted actor born Bernard Schwartz but famous for his screen name. She gained fame as a star of horror films and uses her father's adopted last name . . . ?

ARTS &
CULTURE

739. ► This noted Jewish author wrote *History of the Jews* . . . ?

PEOPLE

740. ► Senator Jacob Javits succeeded this Jewish New York Senator . . . ?

RELIGION

741. ► A *Machzor* is used on . . . ?

HISTORY

742. ► The Haganah began by representing the entire Jewish community of Palestine. Two new organizations subsequently evolved from its membership. What were they?

LANGUAGE

743. ► The *Yiddish* expression *nu* translates into the English exclamation . . . ?

GEOGRAPHY

744. ► This Mideast nation recently expelled 100,000 Arabs from a neighboring country, prohibited them from taking their savings, and promised them higher wages if they converted their citizenship . . . ?

(Answers next page.)

ANSWERS

737. ► 2.5 percent.

738. ► Jamie Lee Curtis (daughter of Tony Curtis).

739. ► Heinrich Graetz.

740. ► Herbert Lehman.

741. ► High Holy Days and for festival prayers.

742. ► The "Irgun" and the "Lechi."

743. ► Well! or So!

744. ► Libya (retaliating against the Egyptian government by abusing Egyptian citizens in Libya).

CURRENT
EVENTS

745. ► During Operation Peace for Galilee he was Israel's Ambassador to the U.N....?

WOMEN

746. ► This French Jewish actress won the 1959 Academy Award for *Room At The Top*...?

ARTS &
CULTURE

747. ► Eliezer ben Yehuda is most noted for this compilation and writing...?

PEOPLE

748. ► *On The Town* and *Kaddish* are among this Jewish composer's most celebrated works...?

RELIGION

749. ► According to the Talmud, this is the best cure-for all ailments...?

HISTORY

750. ► Recalling his visit to the Hurva Synagogue in Jerusalem in 1920, this Englishman said: "That day, they saw for the first time since the destruction of the Temple, a Governor in the land of Palestine who was one of their people. They saw it as the fulfillment of an ancient prophecy...?"

LANGUAGE

751. ► The Talmudic title Rabenu means...?

GEOGRAPHY

752. ► Most of America's earliest Reform Jews come from this country...?

ANSWERS

CURRENT
EVENTS **745.** ▶ **Yehuda Blum.**

WOMEN **746.** ▶ **Simone Signoret.**

ARTS &
CULTURE **747.** ▶ **The Dictionary of Ancient and Modern Hebrew (Ehud Ben-Yehuda's pocket dictionary).**

PEOPLE **748.** ▶ **Leonard Bernstein.**

RELIGION **749.** ▶ **Studying the Torah.**

HISTORY **750.** ▶ **Sir Herbert Samuel (first High Commissioner of Palestine).**

LANGUAGE **751.** ▶ **Our Master or our Teacher. (It was given to Patriarchs and Presidents of the Sanhedrin.)**

GEOGRAPHY **752.** ▶ **Germany.**

CURRENT
EVENTS

753. ► This non-Zionist, extremely religious Israeli political party has been part of both the Labor and Likud governments and is currently represented in Israel's Unity Government . . . ?

WOMEN

754. ► Molly Picon and Gertrude Berg both started their acting careers in this ethnic genre . . . ?

ARTS &
CULTURE

755. ► In what publication is the first printed history of the Jews in the United States found?

PEOPLE

756. ► Bobby Fischer beat this Soviet Jew for the Chess Championship of the world . . . ?

RELIGION

757. ► The Talmud calls this Jewish holiday "One long day" . . . ?

HISTORY

758. ► In the Paris Peace Conference of 1919, what Agreement regarding the future of the Palestine area was abandoned?

LANGUAGE

759. ► The Yiddish adjective *oysgematert* means . . . ?

GEOGRAPHY

760. ► This city is the highest in Israel . . . ?

ANSWERS

CURRENT
EVENTS   753. ▶ "Agudath Israel."

WOMEN   754. ▶ The Yiddish theater.

ARTS &
CULTURE   755. ▶ The "Farmer's Almanac." (The 1793
edition mentions Jews but much of the
information was incorrect or anti-Semitic.)

PEOPLE   756. ▶ Boris Spassky.

RELIGION   757. ▶ "Rosh Hashanah."

HISTORY   758. ▶ The Sykes-Picot Agreement (for the re-
distribution of land in the former Otto-
man Empire).

LANGUAGE   759. ▶ Fatigued.

GEOGRAPHY   760. ▶ Safed (at 960 meters).

CURRENT
EVENTS

761. ► This major political event occurred in Israel in September, 1983...?

WOMEN

762. ► This Jewish woman was one of the first American civilians to be convicted of spying...?

ARTS &
CULTURE

763. ► This artist is best known for her massive abstract sculpture. Her famous *Homage to the Six Million* is in the collection of the Israel Museum...?

PEOPLE

764. ► What did David Raziel distinguish himself doing?

RELIGION

765. ► "The Beast," mentioned in the Book of Revelation, is interpreted by some as referring to this modern superpower ...?

HISTORY

766. ► What was the argument used by a 17th century Rabbi to persuade Cromwell to allow the Jews to re-enter England?

LANGUAGE

767. ► The Hebrew-Yiddish word *Golem* means...?

GEOGRAPHY

768. ► Roman Vishniac created a photo-journal about this country before the Holocaust...?

ANSWERS

CURRENT EVENTS **761.** ► The resignation of Prime Minister Menachem Begin.

WOMEN **762.** ► Ethel Rosenberg (and her husband Julius).

ARTS & CULTURE **763.** ► Louis Nevelson.

PEOPLE **764.** ► Commanding the "Irgun Zvei Leumi" (or "Etzel").

RELIGION **765.** ► The Soviet Union.

HISTORY **766.** ► The Book of David prophesied that there could be no redemption until the Jews had been scattered from one end of the earth to the other and, therefore, until they were allowed back into England there could never be a "Last Judgement."

LANGUAGE **767.** ► A lifeless creation or a clay figure that cannot speak.

GEOGRAPHY **768.** ► Poland. (It was called "A Vanished World.")

CURRENT
EVENTS

769. ► This country is presently Israel's new partner in scientific research, paying over 3 million dollars annually to Israel for research in such fields as biotechnology, energy, water treatment, computers, and lasers...?

WOMEN

770. ► The 1911 fire that killed 146 garment workers, most of them young Jewish women, became known as...?

ARTS &
CULTURE

771. ► His was a great Jewish voice—distinguished as both a cantor and in opera ...?

PEOPLE

772. ► He was the first president of Hebrew University...?

RELIGION

773. ► The ten plagues are mentioned in the Bible and in this other liturgical book ...?

HISTORY

774. ► In 1952, Israel was shaken by a national debate over this painful and controversial foreign policy question related to WW II...?

LANGUAGE

775. ► This Hebrew letter also represents the number one (1)...?

GEOGRAPHY

776. ► In Biblical times the term Diaspora referred to this place...?

ANSWERS

CURRENT
EVENTS

777. ► This Arab leader was welcomed with a 19-gun salute when he recently visited Red China...?

WOMEN

778. ► The Jewish radical philosopher Emma Goldman was famous for a brand of philosophy which generally resulted in...?

ARTS &
CULTURE

779. ► Elie Wiesel's new 1985 Holocaust novel is called...?

PEOPLE

780. ► He was the venerable Jewish Conductor of the Boston Pops Orchestra...?

RELIGION

781. ► The *mitzvah of Bikur Cholim* means ...?

HISTORY

782. ► This organization was formed in 1939 to coordinate the fundraising activities of: the United Palestine Appeal, the American Joint Distribution Committee, and the National Refugee Service...?

LANGUAGE

783. ► The Yiddish word *handlen* means to...?

GEOGRAPHY

784. ► In recent history, Jewish agricultural settlements were started in this non-Mideast location...?

     (Answers next page.)

ANSWERS

CURRENT EVENTS 777. ► Yasir Arafat.

WOMEN 778. ► Anarchy.

ARTS & CULTURE 779. ► "The Fifth Son." (About the revenge of a survivor's son.)

PEOPLE 780. ► Arthur Fiedler.

RELIGION 781. ► Visitation of the ill and infirm. (This is a highly personal "Mitzvah." Bikur Cholim societies exist in every U.S. city.)

HISTORY 782. ► The United Jewish Appeal.

LANGUAGE 783. ► Haggle over price or to do business.

GEOGRAPHY 784. ► Argentina.

CURRENT
EVENTS

785. ► This former president of Israel was arrested by the KGB while visiting Jews in Moscow . . . ?

WOMEN

786. ► This Jewish film star was the first sex symbol in movie history . . . ?

ARTS &
CULTURE

787. ► What book did Pearl S. Buck write about the Chinese Jewish Community?

PEOPLE

788. ► He was President Kennedy's Jewish Secretary of Health and later became a U.S. Senator . . . ?

RELIGION

789. ► Name the two largest Hassidic groups in the United States . . . ?

HISTORY

790. ► When was the first Israel-Egypt "peace agreement" signed?

LANGUAGE

791. ► The Yiddish expressions *Goyishe Kop* and *Goyishe mazel* mean . . . ?

GEOGRAPHY

792. ► What is the approximate Jewish population of Puerto Rico?

ANSWERS

CURRENT
EVENTS

793. ► The supreme irony in the negotiations with *Shiite* terrorists holding U.S. hostages from the Athens airport hijacking was...?

WOMEN

794. ► In 1972, Sally Priesand achieved acclaim in the Reform movement for this reason...?

ARTS &
CULTURE

795. ► The Billy Rose Sculpture Garden is next to this Museum in Israel...?

PEOPLE

796. ► He was the Chief Prosecutor in Adolf Eichmann's trial...?

RELIGION

797. ► What is the main effect of Reform Judaism on "Jewish ceremonial practices"?

HISTORY

798. ► The UN divided Palestine into what eventually became Israel and Jordan in this year...?

LANGUAGE

799. ► The commonly used Yiddish word to describe a fine and admirable person is...?

GEOGRAPHY

800. ► During World War II, this European country—which had long been considered an enemy of the Jews due to its anti-Semitic history—saved many from death at the hands of the Nazis ...?

ANSWERS

CURRENT EVENTS
793. ▶ The elevation and rehabilitation of Syrian President Assad from the status of a leading supporter of terrorism to heroic protector of U.S. citizens and world peace.

WOMEN
794. ▶ She became their first female rabbi.

ARTS & CULTURE
795. ▶ The Israel Museum.

PEOPLE
796. ▶ Gideon Hausner.

RELIGION
797. ▶ It simplifies and dispenses with those traditions that, according to Reform interpretations, lack contemporary importance.

HISTORY
798. ▶ 1947 (November 29th).

LANGUAGE
799. ▶ A "mensch."

GEOGRAPHY
800. ▶ Spain. (Many Sephardic Jews who had previously applied for Spanish citizenship or who had appeared on embassy lists as former Spanish subjects were saved. Some families had not visited Spain for 500 years.)

CURRENT
EVENTS
801. ► He replaced Samuel Lewis in 1985 as the U.S. Ambassador to Israel...?

WOMEN
802. ► She was a world-renowned radical female Jewish playwright...?

ARTS &
CULTURE
803. ► This popular American sport is not played in Israel...?

PEOPLE
804. ► This Jewish author started the growth industry of "futurism" with his 1970 bestseller...?

RELIGION
805. ► When Israel was part of the Roman Empire, why did the sages change the time of the *Shofar* blowing from the morning to the evening?

HISTORY
806. ► The PLO was founded in this year...?

LANGUAGE
807. ► The Hebrew and Yiddish word *Melamed* translates to...?

GEOGRAPHY
808. ► How would power be generated in the Mediterranean to the Dead Sea canal-project that has been halted due to lack of funding?

ANSWERS

CURRENT
EVENTS   801. ► **Thomas Pickering.**

WOMEN   802. ► **Lillian Hellman.**

ARTS &
CULTURE   803. ► **Ice hockey (for good reason: no ice).**

PEOPLE   804. ► **Alvin Toffler in"Future Shock."**

RELIGION   805. ► **Suspicious Roman authorities, fearful of Jewish uprisings, once interpreted the morning Shofar blasts as a call to arms—so they attacked a synagogue, killing all of the worshippers.**

HISTORY   806. ► **1964.**

LANGUAGE   807. ► **A teacher or a wise man.**

GEOGRAPHY   808. ► **From the more than 1,000-feet drop from Mediterranean Sea level to Dead Sea Level.**

CURRENT
EVENTS

809. ► Israeli demographers estimate that by the year 2025 the Jewish population of the diaspora will drop to (within the nearest million)...?

WOMEN

810. ► Alfred and Francis Hackett wrote the Broadway version of this famous Holocaust story about a young Jewish female...?

ARTS &
CULTURE

811. ► He is referred to as the "Poet of the Hebraic Renaissance"...?

PEOPLE

812. ► He founded Israel's nationalist *Herut* party, the major political party in the *Likud* bloc...?

RELIGION

813. ► Under the provisions of Israel's "Anti-Autopsy Law", under what circumstances is an autopsy permitted?

HISTORY

814. ► Bedouin shepherds discovered how many 2,000-year-old Dead Sea Scrolls?

LANGUAGE

815. ► In both Yiddish and Hebrew the word *letz* means one who is...?

GEOGRAPHY

816. ► This town, once a great seat of Jewish learning, is the oldest in the Upper Galilee...?

ANSWERS

CURRENT EVENTS   **809.** ▶ 5 million people.

WOMEN   **810.** ▶ "The Diary of Anne Frank."

ARTS & CULTURE   **811.** ▶ Chaim Nachman Bialik.

PEOPLE   **812.** ▶ Menachem Begin.

RELIGION   **813.** ▶ When necessary to save a human life, or when authorized by the deceased's next-of-kin.

HISTORY   **814.** ▶ Seven (in 1947).

LANGUAGE   **815.** ▶ A cynic or a comic.

GEOGRAPHY   **816.** ▶ Safed.

CURRENT
EVENTS

817. ► Representatives of the Orthodox community in Israel have called for a law which would ban the raising, marketing and sale of this food...?

WOMEN

818. ► King Solomon was alleged to have had an "affair" with this African queen...?

ARTS &
CULTURE

819. ► This movie dealing with Jewish customs and traditions is the most "Jewish" mass-market-oriented movie ever made...?

PEOPLE

820. ► This Jewish film maker directed *Funny Girl, The Pawnbroker* and *Tootsie* ...?

RELIGION

821. ► Jews that converted to Christianity against their will were known as...?

HISTORY

822. ► The "Righteous of the Nations" refers to whom?

LANGUAGE

823. ► What does *Torah* mean?

GEOGRAPHY

824. ► According to tradition, the geographic location known as "Elijah's Cave" is where the Prophet Elijah took shelter during his flight from the King of Israel. Where in Israel is this Jewish holy site?

ANSWERS

817. ► Pork.

818. ► The Queen of Sheba. (This is one explanation for the existence of Ethiopian Jews.)

819. ► "The Chosen."

820. ► Sidney Lumet.

821. ► "The Marranos."

822. ► The individuals and governments that helped save Jewish lives during the Holocaust.

823. ► Law.

824. ► In Haifa on Mt. Carmel.

CURRENT
EVENTS

825. ► This very prestigious university located in Jerusalem, celebrated it 60th anniversary in 1985...?

WOMEN

826. ► She is a prominent Jewish film and drama critic, based in New York City, with a very un-Jewish sounding, adopted last name...?

ARTS &
CULTURE

827. ► This Jewish author wrote: *The Victim, Herzog, Humboldt's Gift* and *Mr. Sammler's Planet*...?

PEOPLE

828. ► This Jewish businessman led CBS through most of its growth...?

RELIGION

829. ► How many types of labor are traditionally prohibited on the Sabbath?

HISTORY

830. ► This Persian king said: "...the Lord, the God of heaven, hath given me, and he has charged me to build a house in Jerusalem, which is in Judah"...?

LANGUAGE

831. ► In Yiddish, the not-so-nice expression *kochleffel* means one who is...?

GEOGRAPHY

832. ► What are the names of the twin lakes which form part of the Suez Canal?

ANSWERS

825. ► The Hebrew University.

826. ► Judith Crist (born Judith Klein).

827. ► Saul Bellow.

828. ► William Paley.

829. ► Thirty-nine.

830. ► Cyrus, when he invited the Jewish people to return to Israel and rebuild the holy Temple.

831. ► A busybody and creates trouble.

832. ► The Great Bitter Lake and the Little Bitter Lake.

CURRENT
EVENTS

833. ► Mt. Scopus is the site where this American Fundamentalist University has plans to build a major new institution . . . ?

WOMEN

834. ► This noted Jewish singer was awarded the Presidential Medal of Freedom by President Carter . . . ?

ARTS &
CULTURE

835. ► In 1972, this Jewish creative genius wrote *Getting Even* and went on to write many other books, screenplays, and much more . . . ?

PEOPLE

836. ► This significant Jewish-born intellectual said, "Religion is the opiate of the masses . . . ?

RELIGION

837. ► *Havdalah* is . . . ?

HISTORY

838. ► Theodor Herzl first visited Jerusalem in this year . . . ?

LANGUAGE

839. ► The 5 Books of Moses were written in this language . . . ?

GEOGRAPHY

840. ► What famous Jewish institution of higher learning is located in the Washington Heights section of New York City?

ANSWERS

CURRENT
EVENTS
  833. ► **Mormon administered Brigham Young University.**

WOMEN
  834. ► **Opera star Beverly Sills (June 6th, 1980).**

ARTS &
CULTURE
  835. ► **Woody Allen.**

PEOPLE
  836. ► **Karl Marx.**

RELIGION
  837. ► **A ceremony to mark the end of the "Sabbath". It is recited on Saturday night when three stars can first be seen in the sky.**

HISTORY
  838. ► **1898.**

LANGUAGE
  839. ► **Hebrew.**

GEOGRAPHY
  840. ► **Yeshiva University.**

CURRENT
EVENTS

841. ► Although Jews represent only 1 percent of the population in Great Britain, they make up what percentage of the membership of the Royal Academy of Science?

WOMEN

842. ► Belva Plain wrote this bestseller; Its theme was the American Jewish woman...?

ARTS &
CULTURE

843. ► Honey is eaten on *challah* especially during this time of the year...?

PEOPLE

844. ► This Jewish composer took Scott Joplin tunes and turned them into an Academy Award-winning film score ...?

RELIGION

845. ► What are the 4 main ingredients of *charoseth*?

HISTORY

846. ► He was a soldier in the British Army nicknamed "Lawrence of Judea" who trained members of the *Haganah* so that they could protect the oil pipeline from Iraq to Haifa...?

LANGUAGE

847. ► The not-so-nice Yiddish and Hebrew term *Kamtsan* means...?

GEOGRAPHY

848. ► A princess from this Arab country was publicly beheaded in 1977, when she attempted to flee the country with her boyfriend, a commoner...?

ANSWERS

841. ► 7 percent.

842. ► "Evergreen."

843. ► From "Rosh Hashanah" to "Yom Kippur."

844. ► Marvin Hamlisch.

845. ► Apples, almonds, cinnamon and wine—mixed together (eaten during the Passover Seder).

846. ► Charles Orde Wingate.

847. ► A stingy tightwad.

848. ► Saudi Arabia.

CURRENT
EVENTS   **849.** ► Stocks in this Israeli industry collapsed in October of 1983...?

WOMEN   **850.** ► Sylvia Tannenbaum wrote this best-selling novel involving a *rebbetzin* and an American Jewish woman...?

ARTS &
CULTURE   **851.** ► This Jewish songwriter and lyricist produced the music for the movie "Reds" and the play "Sweeney Todd"...?

PEOPLE   **852.** ► This Jewish-born New York City power broker-politician, threatened to sue the publisher of the *Encyclopedia Judaica* if his name appeared in a biographical sketch of prominent American Jews...?

RELIGION   **853.** ► What is the name of the ceremony performed at the end of each Sabbath with wine, candles and spices?

HISTORY   **854.** ► In 1917, British troops entered Jerusalem during this Jewish holiday...?

LANGUAGE   **855.** ► The often-used Yiddish expression *rachmones (pronounced rahkh-maw-ness)* means...?

GEOGRAPHY   **856.** ► In 1903, English politician, Joseph Chamberlain, suggested the creation of a Jewish State based in this location...?

ANSWERS

CURRENT
EVENTS
849. ► The banking industry. (There is currently a major investigation of this scandal which cost thousands of investors millions of dollars.)

WOMEN
850. ► "Rachel, The Rabbi's Wife".

ARTS &
CULTURE
851. ► Steven Sondheim.

PEOPLE
852. ► Robert Moses (although born a Jew, he did not like to think of himself as Jewish).

RELIGION
853. ► "Havdalah."

HISTORY
854. ► Chanukah.

LANGUAGE
855. ► To have compassion or understanding for someone.

GEOGRAPHY
856. ► The country that is currently known as Uganda.

CURRENT
EVENTS

857. ► The terrorists who murdered Israeli athletes at the Munich Olympics called themselves...?

WOMEN

858. ► Gloria Steinem was one of the founders of this magazine...?

ARTS &
CULTURE

859. ► This Jewish author wrote *The Chosen* and *My Name Is Asher Lev*...?

PEOPLE

860. ► This Jewish-born Pope institutionalized celibacy for priests of the Roman Catholic Church...?

RELIGION

861. ► On what holiday is it traditional to wear white?

HISTORY

862. ► When the United States of America gained its independence, how many Jews lived in the new nation?

LANGUAGE

863. ► The much-used Yiddish verb *essen* means...?

GEOGRAPHY

864. ► In the early 1800's, this island nation became the first British possession to grant full political emancipation to it's Jewish citizens...?

ANSWERS

CURRENT EVENTS   857. ▶ **The Black September Movement.**

WOMEN   858. ▶ **MS Magazine.**

ARTS & CULTURE   859. ▶ **Chaim Potok.**

PEOPLE   860. ▶ **Pope Gregory.**

RELIGION   861. ▶ **Yom Kippur.**

HISTORY   862. ▶ **About 2500 (in 1776).**

LANGUAGE   863. ▶ **To eat.**

GEOGRAPHY   864. ▶ **Barbados.**

CURRENT
EVENTS

865. ► This former *Likud* Defense Minister was closer to Anwar Sadat than any other Israeli leader . . . ?

WOMEN

866. ► Alix Kates Shulman wrote this best-seller about American Jewish women . . . ?

ARTS &
CULTURE

867. ► Dr. Philip Birnbaum wrote many books of this type . . . ?

PEOPLE

868. ► *Zalman, or the Madness of God* was a play by this noted Jewish author who is better known for his books than his plays . . . ?

RELIGION

869. ► On which holiday is a *lulav*, or willow-branch, used?

HISTORY

870. ► In this year, King Ferdinand ordered the Jews of Spain to either convert to Christianity or be expelled . . . ?

LANGUAGE

871. ► What if anything is the difference between *kishka* and stuffed derma?

GEOGRAPHY

872. ► On May 15, 1948, which 6 Arab armies attacked and invaded the new State of Israel?

ANSWERS

CURRENT
EVENTS

873. ► Vice-Premier Yitzhak Shamir recently suggested the death penalty be instituted for this crime...?

WOMEN

874. ► Aviva Cantor and Susan Weidman Schneider are both editors of this unique magazine...?

ARTS &
CULTURE

875. ► The stereotypical Jewish American Princess was the heroine of the 1955 novel *Marjorie Morningstar* written by ...?

PEOPLE

876. ► This Jewish actor plays TV's Felix Unger...?

RELIGION

877. ► A difference between the ancient Temple and an ordinary synagogue is...?

HISTORY

878. ► The British called these Jewish freedom fighters the Stern Gang, but they were also known by this other name...?

LANGUAGE

879. ► The Yiddish expression "Gay feifen af'n yam!" means...?

GEOGRAPHY

880. ► The gold-domed Shrine of the "Bahai" faith is located in this Israeli city...?

ANSWERS

CURRENT
EVENTS   **873.** ► **Terrorism.**

WOMEN   **874.** ► **"Lilith," a Jewish feminist magazine.**

ARTS &
CULTURE   **875.** ► **Herman Wouk.**

PEOPLE   **876.** ► **Tony Randall.**

RELIGION   **877.** ► **The Temple was in Jerusalem, synagogues could be anywhere that Jews were.**

HISTORY   **878.** ► **Fighters for the Freedom of Israel or "Lohamei Herut Yisrael" (LEHI).**

LANGUAGE   **879.** ► **Go whistle on the ocean.**

GEOGRAPHY   **880.** ► **In Haifa (on Mt. Carmel).**

CURRENT EVENTS

881. ► Which country in the Middle East has the highest literacy rate?

WOMEN

882. ► Stella Adler ran this world renowned school...?

ARTS & CULTURE

883. ► This Israeli author wrote the bestselling guidebook on Israel's history...?

PEOPLE

884. ► This wealthy American Jewish family owns, among other things, the Hyatt Hotel chain and McCall's Magazine ...?

RELIGION

885. ► This event is recalled annually in the Feast of Lights on Chanukah...?

HISTORY

886. ► The Western Wall was recaptured by the Israeli Army during this month and in this year...?

LANGUAGE

887. ► The Yiddish adjective *pitsel* means...?

GEOGRAPHY

888. ► From what location did ships bring gold, silver and ivory to King Solomon?

ANSWERS

881. ► Israel (87.5 %).

882. ► The Stella Adler Acting School.

883. ► Ze'ev Vilnay ("Israel Guide").

884. ► The Pritzker family of Chicago.

885. ► The triumph of Judah the Maccabee over Antiochus, in 164 C.E. (The Temple was cleansed and Jewish worship restored.)

886. ► June, 1967 (June 7th).

887. ► Little.

888. ► Ophir.

CURRENT
EVENTS
889. ► In 1985, this event wreaked havoc in the office of the White House liaison to the Jewish community, Marshall Breger . . . ?

WOMEN
890. ► She is the most prominent Israeli feminist...?

ARTS &
CULTURE
891. ► This rabbi and prolific author of numerous Judaica books is best known for *The Jewish Book of Why* and *The Second Jewish Book of Why* . . . ?

PEOPLE
892. ► This Jewish psychologist and columnist hosted a TV talk show and wrote the book *What Every Woman Should Know About Men* . . . ?

RELIGION
893. ► What is the main theme of the Book of Lamentations?

HISTORY
894. ► This religious group founded the holy cities of Mecca and Medina . . . ?

LANGUAGE
895. ► The Yiddish word for beautiful is . . . ?

GEOGRAPHY
896. ► Where and what is Tiran?

ANSWERS

CURRENT
EVENTS

889. ► President Reagan's decision to visit the German military cemetery at Bitburg—evoking the wrath of the world Jewish community.

WOMEN

890. ► Marcia Freedman.

ARTS &
CULTURE

891. ► Alfred J. Kolatch.

PEOPLE

892. ► Dr. Joyce Brothers.

RELIGION

893. ► The destruction of Jerusalem and the unhappy implications of this for the Jewish people.

HISTORY

894. ► The Jews.

LANGUAGE

895. ► "Shayn."

GEOGRAPHY

896. ► A small island at the mouth of the Gulf of Eilat which controls navigation into the Red Sea. (The Egyptian blockade of the Straits of Tiran caused the 1967 Six-Day War.)

CURRENT
EVENTS

897. ► The International Olympic Committee sanctions these Israeli Olympic Games, known as . . . ?

WOMEN

898. ► This Jewish entertainer was born Frances Rox and her trademark is her famous TV kiss . . . ?

ARTS &
CULTURE

899. ► This widely-read author is also a rabbi and wrote *When Bad Things Happen to Good People* . . . ?

PEOPLE

900. ► This member of an illustrious philanthropic American Jewish family became the first Jewish United States Senator in the 20th century . . . ?

RELIGION

901. ► Why does one chant when reading the Torah?

HISTORY

902. ► Adolph Hitler came to power in this year . . . ?

LANGUAGE

903. ► The Christian world measures years according to the abbreviation A.D., meaning *Anno Domini* — while the Jewish equivalent is . . . ?

GEOGRAPHY

904. ► French philanthropist Baron Maurice de Hirsch, suggested the creation of a Jewish state based in this location and offered to finance the emigration of Russia's Jews there . . . ?

ANSWERS

897. ► The "Maccabiah Games." (They are held every four years and are open to Jewish athletes from every nation.)

898. ► Dinah Shore.

899. ► Harold S. Kushner.

900. ► U.S. Senator Simon Guggenheim (elected to represent Colorado).

901. ► Because of the injunction to read the Law pleasantly.

902. ► 1933.

903. ► C.E. or the Common Era.

904. ► An area within Argentina.

CURRENT
EVENTS   905. ► What was so embarrassing to the United States about the recent Israeli reprisal raid in Tunisia which leveled the P.L.O.'s headquarters there?

WOMEN   906. ► This Jewish female ventriloquist worked with a puppet called Lamb-chop...?

ARTS &
CULTURE   907. ► His autobiography is titled *New York Jew*...?

PEOPLE   908. ► In 1967, this Israeli politician, seeking a strong leader during the Six-Day War, publicly attempted to persuade his long-time political enemy, David Ben-Gurion, to become the Prime Minister ...?

RELIGION   909. ► Name the three sections of the Bible ...?

HISTORY   910. ► On March 22, 1971, 1200 Jews were arrested at a protest in Washington, D.C. What was their crime?

LANGUAGE   911. ► A *Shabbos Goy* is...?

GEOGRAPHY   912. ► This large city, bordering Tel Aviv, was largely Arab prior to 1948...?

ANSWERS

905. ► It was the U.S. that pressured Tunisia to absorb some P.L.O. forces after they were forced to leave Lebanon in 1982. (When President Reagan supported Israel's right to punish the terrorists wherever they were—he further angered the Tunisian government.)

WOMEN 906. ► Shari Lewis.

ARTS &
CULTURE 907. ► Alfred Kazin.

PEOPLE 908. ► Minister Without Portfolio Menachem Begin.

RELIGION 909. ► The Pentateuch (Torah), the Prophets (Neviim) and the Hagiographa (Ketuvim).

HISTORY 910. ► Disturbing the peace. They blocked the streets in front of the Soviet Embassy to protest the persecution of Soviet Jewry.

LANGUAGE 911. ► A gentile hired to perform tasks prohibited for Jews to do on the Sabbath.

GEOGRAPHY 912. ► Jaffa.

CURRENT
EVENTS

913. ► What two actions did Egypt take in 1967 to provoke the Six-Day War?

WOMEN

914. ► The character created by Shakespeare named Shylock had a daughter who was called . . . ?

ARTS &
CULTURE

915. ► This best-selling Jewish author wrote QB VII . . . ?

PEOPLE

916. ► These Jewish brothers built the largest theater empire in America, controlling at one time over 100 theaters . . . ?

RELIGION

917. ► This religious writing is the major source of Jewish Mysticism from Medieval times to the present . . . ?

HISTORY

918. ► Jewish immigration to Palestine was restricted in 1939 due to the British government's policy—stated in this infamous declaration . . . ?

LANGUAGE

919. ► Lebanon's radical *Hezbollah* party translates in English to . . . ?

GEOGRAPHY

920. ► The notorious anti-Semitic cleric, Archbishop Valerian Trifa, was recently expelled by the U.S. for his wartime activities in the fascist Iron Guard in Rumania. Only this romance-language nation would accept him . . . ?

     (Answers next page.)

ANSWERS

CURRENT
EVENTS
913. ► They ordered all UN forces out of the Sinai and seized the Straits of Tiran with the avowed purpose of stopping all maritime traffic to the major Israeli port of Eilat.

WOMEN
914. ► Jessica.

ARTS &
CULTURE
915. ► Leon Uris.

PEOPLE
916. ► The Schuberts.

RELIGION
917. ► The "Zohar."

HISTORY
918. ► The White Paper.

LANGUAGE
919. ► The Party of God.

GEOGRAPHY
920. ► Portugal. (The government claims that if he is a Nazi war criminal they will immediately expel him. If this should happen, Greece has reportedly agreed to accept him.)

CURRENT
EVENTS

921. ► The Arab "Force Seventeen" was recently formed to guard this controversial leader who is presently being threatened by fellow terrorists...?

WOMEN

922. ► This Jewish author wrote *Up The Down Staircase* and was the granddaughter of Sholom Aleichem...?

ARTS &
CULTURE

923. ► What award did Yehuda Amichai, the noted Israeli writer receive in 1982?

PEOPLE

924. ► Which Arab President was responsible for these quotes in the 1960's: "The Arab national aim is the elimination of Israel," and "We believe that the evil which was placed in the heart of the Arab World should be eradicated."...?

RELIGION

925. ► How many versions of the Ten Commandments are there in the Bible?

HISTORY

926. ► These deceased Israelis have all distinguished themselves in the same way: Jacob Bokai, Havakook Cohen, Shalom Salah Shalom, Joseph Basr and Haim Zarfati...?

LANGUAGE

927. ► This flat circular bread-like roll has an indentation in its middle and is sprinkled with flour and onion...?

GEOGRAPHY

928. ► During the American Revolution there was a company of Jewish patriot militia led by Richard Lushington, who were all residents of this southern city known for its large early Jewish population...?

ANSWERS

921. ► Yassir Arafat (it is his personal group of bodyguards).

922. ► Belle Kaufman.

923. ► He won the Israeli Prize for Literature.

924. ► President Nasser of Egypt (speaking to the President of Iraq and to King Hussein of Jordan).

925. ► Two (one in Exodus 20, and one in Deuteronomy 5).

926. ► They were all Mossad agents and all of them died while on sensitive spy missions.

927. ► A bialy.

928. ► Charleston, South Carolina.

CURRENT
EVENTS
929. ► In fiscal year 1985, the U.S. government provided Israel this amount of American military aid (within 10 percent accuracy)...?

WOMEN
930. ► The women's Zionist organization is better known by this other name...?

ARTS &
CULTURE
931. ► This recent book by Amos Oz was made into a movie...?

PEOPLE
932. ► This Jewish sportscaster, who began his career as a lawyer, said in a recent interview with Barbara Walters, "I know that wherever I go—someone will be out to get me—because I am a Jew."...?

RELIGION
933. ► What is "Halacha"?

HISTORY
934. ► Israel's secret rescue operation that airlifted the Jews of Yemen to the Jewish State was called...?

LANGUAGE
935. ► The Yiddish phrase *gehakteh tsores* refers to one who is...?

GEOGRAPHY
936. ► These two non-Middle East countries controlled the only Jewish settlements in Palestine, before Israeli statehood ...?

     (Answers next page.)

ANSWERS

929. ▶ 1.8 billion dollars.

WOMEN

930. ▶ Hadassah.

ARTS & CULTURE

931. ▶ My Michael.

PEOPLE

932. ▶ Howard Cosell.

RELIGION

933. ▶ Jewish religious law. (Halacha deals with religious practice and observance.)

HISTORY

934. ▶ "Operation Magic Carpet."

LANGUAGE

935. ▶ In total misery.

GEOGRAPHY

936. ▶ France and England.

CURRENT EVENTS
937. ► A commemorative postage stamp was issued in 1985 in honor of the 100th birthday of Dr. Bernard Revel, the first president of this American University...?

WOMEN
938. ► How many daughters did Tevye have in *Fiddler On The Roof*?

ARTS & CULTURE
939. ► This noted Jewish author wrote *A Beggar in Jerusalem* and *The Golem*...?

PEOPLE
940. ► This successful English Jewish banker was asked by British rulers to break the stranglehold that usurious Christian money lenders had in Europe. He was knighted by William III...?

RELIGION
941. ► What do the letters "KT" found on the curtain which covers the Ark in a synagogue stand for?

HISTORY
942. ► From 1948 to 1985 the U.S. has provided approximately how many billions in financial assistance to Israel (within 10 percent accuracy)...?

LANGUAGE
943. ► Survivors of the Holocaust who stayed in Europe after World War II were called D.P.s, which means...?

GEOGRAPHY
944. ► In which geographic region does most of Israel's Arab population reside?

ANSWERS

CURRENT EVENTS	**937.** ▶	**Yeshiva University.**
WOMEN	**938.** ▶	**Five.**
ARTS & CULTURE	**939.** ▶	**Elie Wiesel.**
PEOPLE	**940.** ▶	**Solomon Medina. (His presence succeeded in forcing down interest rates.)**
RELIGION	**941.** ▶	**"Keter Torah" or The Crown of the Law.**
HISTORY	**942.** ▶	**31 billion dollars. ($10 billion in economic assistance and $21 billion in military assistance. Sixty percent of this amount has been in the form of grants.)**
LANGUAGE	**943.** ▶	**Displaced Persons .**
GEOGRAPHY	**944.** ▶	**The northernmost section.**

CURRENT
EVENTS

945. ► Prime Minister Shimon Peres has suggested that West Bank towns and villages should have Palestinian mayors rather than. . . ?

WOMEN

946. ► This Jewish actress played Yetta Marmelstein. . . ?

ARTS &
CULTURE

947. ► These two Jewish authors wrote *The Nine Questions People Ask About Judaism* and *Why The Jews*. . . ?

PEOPLE

948. ► This famous American jurist identified the three necessary ingredients for the realization of Zionism: "Men, money and discipline". . . ?

RELIGION

949. ► For what holiday are candles lit near the Bimah by all members of the Congregation, to memorialize their departed?

HISTORY

950. ► In 1915, something happened to Leo Frank that shocked the Jewish world. In 1985, Frank's name came up again during the controversial testimony of an elderly man who was an eyewitness. He stated. . . ?

LANGUAGE

951. ► A *Tzaddik* is the Yiddish word for. . . ?

GEOGRAPHY

952. ► Over the past ten years, which three American cities have had the largest number of Soviet Jewish immigrants . . . ?

ANSWERS

945. ► Israeli civilian administrators (as has been the case in recent years).

946. ► Barbra Streisand.

947. ► Joseph Telushkin and Dennis Prager.

948. ► U.S. Supreme Court Justice Louis Brandeis.

949. ► The Day of Atonement.

950. ► That Leo Frank was falsely accused of the murder of 14-year-old Mary Phagan and he named the true murderer. (In 1915, Frank was hanged by an angry lynch mob in Atlanta, Georgia. The governor was recently petitioned by national Jewish organizations to clear Frank's name—but no action has been taken as of 1985.)

951. ► A righteous person, a person noted for his faith and piety.

952. ► New York City, Los Angeles, Philadelphia, Chicago, and Miami (in order of population).

CURRENT
EVENTS

953. ► These two European countries were active in the development of Iraq's nuclear reactor . . . ?

WOMEN

954. ► This old-time Jewish actress portrayed the character "Baby Snooks" . . . ?

ARTS &
CULTURE

955. ► This 1981 film, staring Sigourney Weaver and William Hurt, was the first negative portrayal of an Israeli in Hollywood history . . . ?

PEOPLE

956. ► What did Chaim Weizmann do for the British government during World War II which caused them to listen to his pleas for a Zionist State?

RELIGION

957. ► Which act is performed during the traditional Jewish wedding ceremony to serve as a symbolic reminder of the destruction of the Temple?

HISTORY

958. ► This Jewish hero of the War of Independence fought with one hand and after the battle of Tel Chai said on his deathbed: "It is good to die for our country . . . ?

LANGUAGE

959. ► The German World War II term *Juden schlayer* means . . . ?

GEOGRAPHY

960 ► Which African nation currently has the largest Jewish population?

ANSWERS

953. ► France and Italy.

954. ► Fanny Brice.

955. ► "Eyewitness" (an Israeli turned out to be the villian in the end).

956. ► He invented an important chemical compound used by the British to manufacture ammunition and explosives during World War II. (This achievement opened additional doors for him.)

957. ► The bridegroom breaks a glass with his foot.

958. ► Joseph Trumpeldor.

959. ► Jew killer.

960. ► Morocco.

CURRENT
EVENTS

961. ► Cracow, Poland, had 60,000 Jews before World War II. The current Jewish population is approximately (to the nearest 100 people)...?

WOMEN

962. ► Ava Gardner and Lana Turner were both married to this Jewish musician ...?

ARTS &
CULTURE

963. ► This Israeli statesman, author and television personality wrote a recent bestselling book...?

PEOPLE

964. ► This Jewish interviewer and newscaster has been referred to as the most intelligent man on American television due to the impressive quality of the interviews he conducts on his evening news program...?

RELIGION

965. ► At what point during the reading of the Purim megillah are congregants enjoined to make noise?

HISTORY

966. ► The Dead Sea Scrolls were discovered during this decade...?

LANGUAGE

967. ► Repentance, a central concept in Judaism, applies to the believer who sins and to the nonbeliever who returns. This person who returns is known as a...?

GEOGRAPHY

968. ► The architects for the Second Temple came from...?

ANSWERS

961. ▶ 200 (their average age is 73; they have no rabbi and most have had no religious education).

962. ▶ Artie Shaw (born Abraham Isaac Arshansky).

963. ▶ Abba Eban, the author of "Heritage: Civilization and the Jews."

964. ▶ Ted Koppel, the host of "Nightline."

965. ▶ At the mention of the name of Haman.

966. ▶ The 1940s (1947).

967. ▶ "Baal Teshuvah."

968. ▶ Phoenicia (present day Lebanon).

CURRENT
EVENTS

969. ► This bigoted, professional anti-Semite peddles racism and hate, mocks the Holocaust and has called Judaism a "gutter religion"...?

WOMEN

970. ► At one time, she was the owner and editor of the *New York Post*...?

ARTS &
CULTURE

971. ► Jewish thinkers Abraham Joshua Heschel, Martin Buber and Franz Rosenzweig were all distinguished in this area...?

PEOPLE

972. ► This Israeli statesman wrote a book entitled *White Nights*, about his imprisonment by the Soviets in Siberia for the "crime" of Zionism...?

RELIGION

973. ► Channa and her seven sons are associated with this holiday...?

HISTORY

974. ► While the Israeli Army won the 1948 War of Independence, they sacrificed some territory during this war. What was lost?

LANGUAGE

975. ► The Yiddish and Ladino alphabets use these types of letters...?

GEOGRAPHY

976. ► The United Nations Partition Plan of 1947 involved dividing Palestine into 3 parts under 3 areas of control. What 3 groups controlled these areas?

ANSWERS

CURRENT
EVENTS 969. ► Louis Farrakhan.

WOMEN 970. ► Dorothy Schiff.

ARTS &
CULTURE 971. ► Philosophy.

PEOPLE 972. ► Former Israeli Prime Minister Menachem Begin.

RELIGION 973. ► Chanukah.

HISTORY 974. ► The Jewish quarter in the Old City of Jerusalem was lost until the 1967 Six-Day War.

LANGUAGE 975. ► Hebrew.

GEOGRAPHY 976. ► The Jews controlled one zone, the Arabs another, and Jerusalem was under U.N. control.

CURRENT EVENTS

977. ► The *Tehiya* Party, a right-wing Israeli political party, was formed as a result of this event...?

WOMEN

978. ► This Jewish female film star was known as "The Vamp"...?

ARTS & CULTURE

979. ► This respected Jewish author wrote the classic *Redemption of the Unwanted*...?

PEOPLE

980. ► He was one of the top Jewish scholars of the modern era and authored *Studies in Judaism*. In 1901, he became president of the Jewish Theological Seminary...?

RELIGION

981. ► Why did Greek and Roman slave-masters consider the Jewish people to be lazy?

HISTORY

982. ► There were no synagogues built in Spain for how many hundreds of years?

LANGUAGE

983. ► One who abandons his or her religious belief is an...?

GEOGRAPHY

984. ► These 2 Middle East nations emerged from the dismantling of the Turkish-Ottoman Empire as initially French controlled areas in 1920, and subsequently independent nations, in 1943 and 1944 respectively...?

ANSWERS

CURRENT EVENTS

977. ► The Camp David Accords (MK Geula Cohen and other leaders who disapproved of the Accords as being "traitorous" to Israel formed "Tehiya". The leadership is composed of former Herut Party members and Gush Emunin).

WOMEN

978. ► Theda Bara (born Theodosia Goodman).

ARTS & CULTURE

979. ► Abraham Sachar.

PEOPLE

980. ► Dr. Solomon S. Schechter (1850-1915).

RELIGION

981. ► Because Judaism required a day of rest for all workers.

HISTORY

982. ► 600 years.

LANGUAGE

983. ► Apostate.

GEOGRAPHY

984. ► Syria (in 1943) and Lebanon (in 1944).

CURRENT
EVENTS

985. ► Raphael Eitan held this position in the Israeli government from 1979 to 1983 ...?

WOMEN

986. ► This Jewish opera star was fondly nick-named "Bubbles"...?

ARTS &
CULTURE

987. ► This innovative Jewish teacher is known as "the father of method acting" ...?

PEOPLE

988. ► On January 7, 1957, this Israeli statesman said, "It is our belief that a great Jewish community, a free Jewish nation, in Palestine, with a large scope for its activities, will be of good benefit to our Arab neighbors. We need each other, we can benefit from each other" ...?

RELIGION

989. ► Why is a lamb bone put on the Passover table?

HISTORY

990. ► In 1964, what did Syria try to do vis-a-vis the Jordan River that angered Israel?

LANGUAGE

991. ► The frequently used Yiddish exclamation *Genug* means...?

GEOGRAPHY

992. ► The historically accurate name for the region known as the West Bank is...?

ANSWERS

985. ► Commander in Chief.

986. ► Beverly Sills.

987. ► Lee Strasberg.

988. ► David Ben-Gurion (responding to the findings of the Peel Commission).

989. ► To symbolize the Paschal lamb that the ancient Hebrews sacrificed before they left Egypt.

990. ► They attempted to divert the Jordan's headwaters. This would cause Israel to lose its main source of fresh water for irrigation purposes. (Israeli artillery destroyed the Syrian equipment involved in this project.)

991. ► Enough.

992. ► Judea and Samaria.

CURRENT EVENTS

993. ► What was the specific Arab rationale behind the 1973 oil embargo?

WOMEN

994. ► Her sons were humorous performers nicknamed "Minnie's Boys"...?

ARTS & CULTURE

995. ► He was the Italian Jewish painter whose trademark was painting women with long necks...?

PEOPLE

996. ► This Jewish author wrote *The Stepford Wives*, *Rosemary's Baby*, and *The Boys from Brazil*...?

RELIGION

997. ► How many meals are traditionally required to be eaten on the Sabbath?

HISTORY

998. ► Which inherently anti-Semitic group attempted to prevent Germany from paying reparations to Jewish victims of the Nazi era?

LANGUAGE

999. ► This Yiddish word refers to a person who is unlucky. It begins with the Yiddish word for luck...?

GEOGRAPHY

1000. ► Name the two Scandinavian countries where no Jews were sent to their deaths during the Nazi era?

 (Answers next page.)

ANSWERS

CURRENT EVENTS **993.** ► They wanted the oil dependent countries to pressure Israel into returning to the 1967 cease-fire lines.

WOMEN **994.** ► The Marx Brothers.

ARTS & CULTURE **995.** ► Modigliani.

PEOPLE **996.** ► Ira Levin.

RELIGION **997.** ► Three.

HISTORY **998.** ► The Arab League (formed in February 1945).

LANGUAGE **999.** ► "Schlimazeldiker."

GEOGRAPHY **1000.** ► Finland and Sweden.

CURRENT
EVENTS   **1001.** ▶ What was Daniel Moynihan referring
to when he said: "The United States will
not abide by; it will not acquiesce in this
infamous act. A great evil has been
loosed upon the world. The abomina-
tion of anti-Semitism has been given
the appearance of international sanc-
tion...?

WOMEN   **1002.** ▶ Marilyn Monroe and Elizabeth Taylor
were both film stars but they also had
this in common...?

ARTS &
CULTURE   **1003.** ▶ The oldest continuously published Jewish periodical is...?

PEOPLE   **1004.** ▶ This Jewish business wizard created the
world's largest cosmetics company
...?

RELIGION   **1005.** ▶ From which direction should Chanukah candles be lit?

HISTORY   **1006.** ▶ Why did Israel withdraw from the
Sinai after the successful 1956 Sinai
Campaign?

LANGUAGE   **1007.** ▶ The Hebrew word for Prayer Book is
...?

GEOGRAPHY **1008.** ▶ The first nation to give Israel *official*,
rather than *de facto*, recognition was
...?

ANSWERS

CURRENT EVENTS 1001. ▶ The UN resolution condemning Zionism as a form of racism.

WOMEN 1002. ▶ They converted to Judaism to marry their Jewish husbands.

ARTS & CULTURE 1003. ▶ The Jewish Chronicle of London (Published since 1841).

PEOPLE 1004. ▶ Charles Revson.

RELIGION 1005. ▶ Left to right.

HISTORY 1006. ▶ Because the UN requested a pull-back to the borders that existed before the war. (The U.S. also applied tremendous pressure forcing Israel to relinquish captured territory.)

LANGUAGE 1007. ▶ "Siddur".

GEOGRAPHY 1008. ▶ The Soviet Union.

CURRENT
EVENTS

1009. ► He was Ariel Sharon's chief legal counsel during the famous trial against *Time* magazine...?

WOMEN

1010. ► "Will you still love me tomorrow," was the refrain to one of the great hits of this Jewish singer...?

ARTS &
CULTURE

1011. ► He wrote the recent book *Ben Gurion: Prophet of Fire*...?

PEOPLE

1012. ► This Jewish psychologist is known as "the father of transactional analysis" ...?

RELIGION

1013. ► When is the "Book of Life" inscribed, and when is it sealed?

HISTORY

1014. ► In response to the 1940 British restrictions on Jewish land purchases, who said, "They confine the Jews within a small pale of settlement similar to that which existed in Czarist Russia...and as now exists only under Nazi rule"?

LANGUAGE

1015. ► The *Haggadah* is written in these two languages...?

GEOGRAPHY

1016. ► The only two nations in the Western Hemisphere to recognize Jerusalem as the capital of Israel are...?

ANSWERS

CURRENT EVENTS	**1009.** ►	**Milton Gould.**
WOMEN	**1010.** ►	**Carole King (it was from her Tapestries album).**
ARTS & CULTURE	**1011.** ►	**Dan Kurzman.**
PEOPLE	**1012.** ►	**Dr. Eric Berne.**
RELIGION	**1013.** ►	**It is inscribed on "Rosh Hashanah," and sealed on "Yom Kippur."**
HISTORY	**1014.** ►	**David Ben-Gurion (on February 28th, 1940).**
LANGUAGE	**1015.** ►	**Hebrew and Aramaic.**
GEOGRAPHY	**1016.** ►	**Costa Rica and El Salvador.**

CURRENT EVENTS **1017.** ► The Chairman of West Berlin's Jewish community recently requested legal action from German Interior Minister Friedrich Zimmermann to ban annual reunions of Nazi SS veterans. The reactions to his pleas were . . . ?

WOMEN **1018.** ► This female Reconstructionist rabbi recently accompanied Eric Strom and his family to Poland for the first *Bar Mitzvah* in Cracow in 35 years . . . ?

ARTS & CULTURE **1019.** ► This family was a dominant force in the field of Hebrew printing for 500 years . . . ?

PEOPLE **1020.** ► In 1940, this Jewish author wrote *Darkness At Noon,* one of the most important personal and political statements in modern literature . . . ?

RELIGION **1021.** ► The three books of the *Hagiographa* are . . . ?

HISTORY **1022.** ► Approximately what percentage of Europe's Jewish population lived in Germany *up until* World War II?

LANGUAGE **1023.** ► The title *Gaon* refers to . . . ?

GEOGRAPHY **1024.** ► These two Jewish edifices were built on Jerusalem's Mount Moriah . . . ?

ANSWERS

1017. ► Rejection of the request because SS veterans were "well behaved" during their reunions and posed no threat to the democratic system.

1018. ► Rabbi Emily Korzenick. (Disputes erupted among Orthodox rabbis there over the prospects of having her participate in services in an Orthodox synagogue.)

1019. ► The Soncino's (the company still operates today in Europe and in the United States under different ownership).

1020. ► Arthur Koestler.

1021. ► Psalms, Proverbs and Job.

1022. ► Less than 5%.

1023. ► An important rabbi.

1024. ► The First and Second Temples.

CURRENT
EVENTS
1025. ► Rudy Boschwitz, a leading Jewish supporter of Israel in the United States Senate, represents this state . . . ?

WOMEN
1026. ► Centuries ago, how would the few rare female Talmudic scholars lecture to men—and still not violate the strict religious laws of their times?

ARTS &
CULTURE
1027. ► In a recently published book, this Jewish author switched from his traditional themes to write *The Golem* . . . ?

PEOPLE
1028. ► This Jewish business wizard made his fortune in Canadian uranium mining and spent his money on the acquisition of art which he frequently donated to the American people . . . ?

RELIGION
1029. ► With which holiday is King Ahasuerus associated?

HISTORY
1030. ► After World War II, a secret group called the Sonneborn Institute was formed by American Zionist Rudolf Sonneborn and others for the purpose of . . . ?

LANGUAGE
1031. ► The *Chanukiah* is another word for . . . ?

GEOGRAPHY
1032. ► Former Israeli Prime Minister Golda Meir was a schoolteacher in this American city . . . ?

(Answers next page.)

ANSWERS

CURRENT EVENTS   **1025.** ▶ **Minnesota (Republican).**

WOMEN   **1026.** ▶ **They would speak from behind a closed door or from behind a screen.**

ARTS & CULTURE   **1027.** ▶ **Elie Wiesel.**

PEOPLE   **1028.** ▶ **Joseph P. Hirshhorn.**

RELIGION   **1029.** ▶ **Purim.**

HISTORY   **1030.** ▶ **Buying and smuggling arms and military equipment to Israel. (The formation of this clandestine American arm of the Hagganah was initiated by Ben-Gurion).**

LANGUAGE   **1031.** ▶ **"Menorah."**

GEOGRAPHY   **1032.** ▶ **Milwaukee, Wisconsin.**

CURRENT EVENTS   **1033.** ► The present Chief Rabbis of Israel pronounced these Jews as being the remnants of the Tribe of Dan...?

WOMEN   **1034.** ► This Jewish actress starred in a late night soap opera and was once married to Woody Allen...?

ARTS & CULTURE   **1035.** ► He compiled and authored *The American Jewish Album: 1654 to the Present*...?

PEOPLE   **1036.** ► This Jewish film magnate donated an original copy of the U.S. Bill of Rights to the Library of Congress...?

RELIGION   **1037.** ► On what traditional day of mourning were the Jews expelled from Spain in 1492?

HISTORY   **1038.** ► In 1945, an Anglo-American Committee of Inquiry was formed to review the dual problems of Jewish immigration and the Holocaust survivors. What was it's recommendation?

LANGUAGE   **1039.** ► Israel's national anthem *Hatikvah*, in English means...?

GEOGRAPHY   **1040.** ► This South American country has the highest percentage of Jews among its population...?

ANSWERS

1033. ▶ The Ethiopian Jews. (Commonly referred to as "Falashas." A perjorative term meaning strangers.)

1034. ▶ Louise Lasser (she starred in Mary Hartman, Mary Hartman).

1035. ▶ Allen Schoener.

1036. ▶ Barney Balaban. (He bought it at an auction in 1945. It is now on display near the U.S. Constitution and the Declaration of Independence.)

1037. ▶ Tisha B'Av, the Fast of the Ninth day of Av.

1038. ▶ "Bi-nationalism" or a single state controlled by Britain. (They also recommended an end to land purchase restrictions and immediate entry of 100,000 Jews.)

1039. ▶ The hope.

1040. ▶ Uruguay (with 50,000 Jews, or 139 Jews per 1000 inhabitants).

CURRENT
EVENTS   1041. ▶ The PLO's treasury is estimated to total...?

WOMEN   1042. ▶ This Jewish actress was the heroine of *Star Wars*...?

ARTS &
CULTURE   1043. ▶ This Israeli literary prize is awarded to the author who best expresses the idea of freedom of the individual in society...?

PEOPLE   1044. ▶ This rabbi was immortalized in a famous Rembrandt etching...?

RELIGION   1045. ▶ In 1824, the Jewish population of this southern city favored altering some Jewish customs and ceremonies in order to make their religious observance more compatible with their surroundings...?

HISTORY   1046. ▶ This American President appointed the first Jew to the U.S. Supreme Court ...?

LANGUAGE   1047. ▶ The Hebrew term *Yekkee* refers to this type of Jew...?

GEOGRAPHY   1048. ▶ This nation is Israel's second largest export partner...?

ANSWERS

CURRENT EVENTS **1041.** ► $5 billion dollars—generating 1 billion dollars per year in revenues. (From *Jewish Week*, August 30th, 1985.)

WOMEN **1042.** ► Carrie Fisher (daughter of Eddie Fisher and Debbie Reynolds).

ARTS & CULTURE **1043.** ► The Jerusalem Prize.

PEOPLE **1044.** ► Rabbi Manassah Ben Israel.

RELIGION **1045.** ► Charleston, South Carolina (Congregation Beth Elohim).

HISTORY **1046.** ► Woodrow Wilson.

LANGUAGE **1047.** ► One of German ethnic background. (It is often used pejoratively to describe one who is very rigid.)

GEOGRAPHY **1048.** ► West Germany.

CURRENT
EVENTS
1049. ► This 1984 Presidential candidate supported government-sponsored prayer, religious meetings in public schools, religious displays on public property and has never been to Israel...?

WOMEN
1050. ► This female Jewish author influenced literary and artistic life of the 1920s and 1930s. Her best known work was the *Autobiography of Alice B. Toklas* ....?

ARTS &
CULTURE
1051. ► This American Jewish intellectual owns and publishes *The New Republic* magazine?

PEOPLE
1052. ► This distinguished Jewish author taught at Sarah Lawrence College and wrote *Loon Lake*, *Ragtime* and *The Book of Daniel*...?

RELIGION
1053. ► What is the major distinction that Reform Judaism makes concerning Jewish Law?

HISTORY
1054. ► He was the first early American Jewish leader to demand equal rights for the Jewish people in the new colonies...?

LANGUAGE
1055. ► The German term *Judenrein*, used frequently during the Holocaust, means ...?

GEOGRAPHY
1056. ► Israel recently destroyed the P.L.O. headquarters in this nation after 3 Israelis were murdered aboard their yacht in Larnaca, Cyprus...?

(Answers next page.)

ANSWERS

1049. ▶ Ronald Reagan.

1050. ▶ Gertrude Stein.

1051. ▶ Martin Peretz (a descendent of I.L. Peretz).

1052. ▶ E. L. Doctorow.

1053. ▶ It emphasizes the Laws which have a universal ethical importance and minimizes the importance of those that apply to particular times and conditions.

1054. ▶ Asser Levy. (He was active in New Amsterdam, now New York City.)

1055. ▶ Free of any Jews.

1056. ▶ Tunisia. (In October 1985, Israeli fighter jets flew 1500 miles and decimated the P.L.O.'s world headquarters. This was Israel's most long range military mission since the Entebbe rescue mission of 1976.)

CURRENT
EVENTS

1057. ► The main reason that Israel's Labor Party opposes expansion of Jewish settlements on the West Bank territories is . . . ?

WOMEN

1058. ► This Jewish feminist wrote a novel about heroine Isadora Wing's conflict between preserving her marriage versus female autonomy . . . ?

ARTS &
CULTURE

1059. ► This large Jewish organization publishes the *Congress Bi-Weekly* and *Commentary* magazine . . . ?

PEOPLE

1060. ► This Jewish High Commissioner to Palestine temporarily halted all Jewish immigration as a reaction to Arab rioting in May of 1921 . . . ?

RELIGION

1061. ► On which holiday is the ceremony of *Tashlich* performed, in which one's sins are symbolically cast away?

HISTORY

1062. ► In 1822, State Assemblyman Thomas Kennedy, a gentile member of his state's legislature, successfully introduced a bill known as Kennedy's "Jew Baby"— which would allow Jews the right to vote. It was eventually enacted into law in this Eastern state . . . ?

LANGUAGE

1063. ► After Israel, the second most active Yiddish center is . . . ?

GEOGRAPHY

1064. ► When, if ever, was Jerusalem the capital city of an Arab country?

(Answers next page.)

ANSWERS

1057. ► Due to concern over the final status of the disputed area. (They believe that ultimately peace talks will be necessary with Jordan and with representative of the Palestinians living there.

WOMEN 1058. ► Erica Jong, "Fear of Flying."

ARTS &
CULTURE 1059. ► The American Jewish Congress.

PEOPLE 1060. ► Sir Herbert Samuel.

RELIGION 1061. ► Rosh Hashanah.

HISTORY 1062. ► Maryland. (He started his struggle in 1804 and after several defeats, achieved his goal in 1825, when the "Jew Bill" was finally passed.)

LANGUAGE 1063. ► Buenos Aires, Argentina.

GEOGRAPHY 1064. ► Never.

Trivia Judaica.   **QUESTIONS**

CURRENT
EVENTS   1065. ► What is the different feature of the
                    recently issued new Israeli Shekel?

WOMEN   1066. ► This female author and editor wrote *The
                    Erotic Life of the American Wife,* accur-
                    ately identifying the changes in female
                    consciousness caused by the feminist and
                    sexual revolutions. Her follow up book
                    *Dominus: A Woman Looks at Men's
                    Lives,* analyzed the effects of these
                    movements on men . . . ?

ARTS &
CULTURE   1067. ► This self-appointed former African
                    emperor called himself *The Lion of
                    Judah*. . . ?

PEOPLE   1068. ► This American Zionist was Treasury
                    Secretary from 1934 to 1945, when he
                    resigned to devote himself exclusively
                    to Jewish affairs. . . ?

RELIGION   1069. ► Haman, the villain of the Purim story,
                    had how many sons?

HISTORY   1070. ► Adolph Cremieux, a famous Jewish
                    French statesman from 1840 to 1880,
                    successfully led a life-long fight for
                    this. . . ?

LANGUAGE   1071. ► In Yiddish, when a person recieves a
                    zetz, they get a . . . ?

GEOGRAPHY   1072. ► The Jordanian government allows Pal-
                    estinian Jews to enter their country un-
                    der what circumstances—if any . . . ?

267   (Answers next page.)

ANSWERS

CURRENT EVENTS 1065. ► It will lose three zeroes (inflation made the old shekel devalue to 1500 per one U.S. dollar).

WOMEN 1066. ► Natalie Gittelson.

ARTS & CULTURE 1067. ► Ethiopia's Haile Selassie.

PEOPLE 1068. ► Henry Morgenthau, Jr.

RELIGION 1069. ► Ten.

HISTORY 1070. ► The fight for equal treatment for the Jews of France (and Jews all over the world).

LANGUAGE 1071. ► Punch.

GEOGRAPHY 1072. ► Palestinian Jews are never allowed legal entry. The Jordanian constitution specifically states that all Palestinians "except Jews" may enter Jordan.

CURRENT EVENTS   **1073.** ► These Mideast and west European nations almost had a military showdown over the occupation of northern Chad . . . ?

WOMEN   **1074.** ► She wrote *On Being A Jewish Feminist* . . . ?

ARTS & CULTURE   **1075.** ► This Jewish author wrote the classic bestsellers *In the Footsteps of the Prophets* and *In the footsteps of Moses* . . . ?

PEOPLE   **1076.** ► Which British statesman said " . . . I hope that . . . they will not grudge that small notch—for it is no more than that geographically, whatever it may be historically—that small notch in what are now Arab territories being given to the people who for all these hundreds of years have been separated from it"?

RELIGION   **1077.** ► This Book of the Bible is read during the *Tisha B'Av* service . . . ?

HISTORY   **1078.** ► This Zionist fighting organization was formed to do battle on the side of the allies in their war with Turkey over the liberation of Palestine . . . ?

LANGUAGE   **1079.** ► The Hebrew acronym *Nili*—stands for this in English . . . ?

GEOGRAPHY   **1080.** ► The only city in Nebraska with over 1,000 Jewish residents is . . . ?

ANSWERS

CURRENT EVENTS   **1073.** ▶ Libya and France.

WOMEN   **1074.** ▶ Susannah Heschel.

ARTS & CULTURE   **1075.** ▶ Moshe Pearlman.

PEOPLE   **1076.** ▶ A.J. Balfour (July 12th, 1920).

RELIGION   **1077.** ▶ The Book of Lamentations.

HISTORY   **1078.** ▶ The "Zion Mule Corps."

LANGUAGE   **1079.** ▶ The Glory of Israel will not die (Netzach Yisroel Lo Yeshaker).

GEOGRAPHY   **1080.** ▶ Omaha. (An estimated 6,500 live there, Lincoln is next with approximately 800.)

CURRENT
EVENTS   1081. ► Pope Paul II shocked the Jewish world
with this official comment about Jeru-
salem...?

WOMEN   1082. ► In Israel's pre-Statehood days, who
was *Aviva Reik*...?

ARTS &
CULTURE   1083. ► The 1984 film *The Little Drummer
Girl* offended many in the Jewish community because of its unpopular portrayal of these two competing forces
...?

PEOPLE   1084. ► This Jewish U.S. Supreme Court Justice
was known as "The People's Attorney"
...?

RELIGION 1085. ► *Lag B'omer* occurs how many days into
the counting of the omer?

HISTORY   1086. ► He was Secretary of State in the days of
the Confederacy...?

LANGUAGE 1087. ► The British government gave this title
to the English ruler of Palestine during
the Mandate period...?

GEOGRAPHY 1088. ► Canada's growing Jewish community
now numbers...?

ANSWERS

1081. ▶ He called for a review of Jerusalem's current status claiming it should not be the capital of the monotheistic religions.

WOMEN 1082. ▶ A secret agent for the "Haganah".

ARTS &
CULTURE 1083. ▶ The sympathetic treatment of the Palestinian position on the Mideast and the negative portrayal of "ruthless, manipulative" Israeli agents.

PEOPLE 1084. ▶ Louis D. Brandeis.

RELIGION 1085. ▶ Thirty-three days.

HISTORY 1086. ▶ Judah P. Benjamin.

LANGUAGE 1087. ▶ High Commissioner.

GEOGRAPHY 1088. ▶ Approximately 345,000.

CURRENT EVENTS **1089.** ► What is the most controversial political position of Knesset member Meir Kahane?

WOMEN **1090.** ► This Sabbath delicacy is often called "Jewish Soul food"...?

ARTS & CULTURE **1091.** ► This Jewish comedian's penchant is to insult people in the audience with his quick sardonic wit...?

PEOPLE **1092.** ► What did Jonas Salk and Albert Sabin discover...?

RELIGION **1093.** ► A food that is neither meat nor dairy is called...?

HISTORY **1094.** ► The Sykes-Picot Agreement, accepted by these two European nations, was the basis for the future of the Palestine area...?

LANGUAGE **1095.** ► The Yiddish expression *Shanda* means ...?

GEOGRAPHY **1096.** ► The recent airlift of Ethiopian Jews was conducted in large part with charter flights on planes from this country...?

(Answers next page.)

ANSWERS

CURRENT EVENTS **1089.** ▶ His advocacy of the expulsion of all Arabs from Israel.

WOMEN **1090.** ▶ "Cholent."

ARTS & CULTURE **1091.** ▶ Don Rickles.

PEOPLE **1092.** ▶ The Polio vaccine.

RELIGION **1093.** ▶ "Parve."

HISTORY **1094.** ▶ Britain and France.

LANGUAGE **1095.** ▶ A shame, a scandal or an embarrassment.

GEOGRAPHY **1096.** ▶ Belgium.

CURRENT
EVENTS   1097. ► Ernst Zundel was sentenced to 15 months in jail by a Canadian court for disseminating racist statements in his outrageous pamphlet that claimed ...?

WOMEN   1098. ► This leading Jewish feminist leader was once a Playboy bunny...?

ARTS &
CULTURE   1099. ► This Jewish actor was the star of *Spartacus*...?

PEOPLE   1100. ► This man has come to be known as the "Jewish Farrakhan"...?

RELIGION   1101. ► A *mezuzah* is always placed on this side of the doorpost...?

HISTORY   1102. ► What precipitated the Israel-Egyptian fighting in the Sinai, during 1956?

LANGUAGE   1103. ► The derogatory Yiddish term *Shmatta* refers to something that is...?

GEOGRAPHY   1104. ► The notorious Auschwitz concentration camp was in this country...?

ANSWERS

CURRENT EVENTS   **1097.** ▶ No Jews had been persecuted or exterminated during WWII (It was titled "Did Six Million Really Die?"

WOMEN   **1098.** ▶ Gloria Steinem.

ARTS & CULTURE   **1099.** ▶ Kirk Douglas.

PEOPLE   **1100.** ▶ Knesset member Meir Kahane for his outspoken extremist position and his racist political views.

RELIGION   **1101.** ▶ The right side.

HISTORY   **1102.** ▶ Egypt sealed the Israeli port of Eilat by blocking the Gulf of Aqaba, preventing the movement of Israeli shipping. Israel regarded this an act act of war.

LANGUAGE   **1103.** ▶ Cheap or junk.

GEOGRAPHY   **1104.** ▶ Poland.

CURRENT
EVENTS
1105. ▶ 1982 was such a turbulent time in Israeli politics that there were two Defense Ministers. Who were they?

WOMEN
1106. ▶ What female author wrote a bestselling *roman a clef* about her disasterous marriage to this Jewish Watergate sleuth?

ARTS &
CULTURE
1107. ▶ Which two Jewish singers played the lead roles in different versions of *The Jazz Singer*?

PEOPLE
1108. ▶ This Jewish lawyer was named to succeed Oliver Wendell Holmes on the United States Supreme Court...?

RELIGION
1109. ▶ This Jewish scholar had not studied until the age of 40 when his wife urged him to go off and learn the *Torah*. He returned 24 years later with 24,000 disciples...?

HISTORY
1110. ▶ In 1940, the British government allowed German Jewish refugees from the ship *St. Louis*—that no other nation would allow on their land—to remain in England. What was unusual about the British government's treatment of these survivors, one year later?

LANGUAGE
1111. ▶ The not-so-nice Yiddish expression *Alter kocker* means...?

GEOGRAPHY
1112. ▶ The capital of the ancient Jewish kingdom of Judea was...?

ANSWERS

CURRENT EVENTS **1105.** ► Ariel Sharon followed by Moshe Arens.

WOMEN **1106.** ► Nora Ephron, the novel is "Heartburn," her former husband is Carl Bernstein.

ARTS & CULTURE **1107.** ► Neil Diamond, new version; and Al Jolson, old version.

PEOPLE **1108.** ► Benjamin N. Cardozo.

RELIGION **1109.** ► Rabbi Akiva.

HISTORY **1110.** ► They were interned as "enemy aliens" and treated as Nazi agents because they were also from Germany. The British government ignored the fact that Jews could not logically be Nazi sysmpathizers.

LANGUAGE **1111.** ► Old fogey or old man.

GEOGRAPHY **1112.** ► Jerusalem.

CURRENT
EVENTS
1113. ► Advocates of lighter sentences for Jews convicted of terrorism use this Israeli government action to support their argument...?

WOMEN
1114. ► This Jewish movie star and singer endowned a chair in Jewish studies in her father's name at a leading American university...?

ARTS &
CULTURE
1115. ► This famous gentile artist portrayed Moses holding the two tablets in a painting...?

PEOPLE
1116. ► This Israeli anthropologist is the author of *Masada Bar-kochba, Hazor* and several books on the Dead Sea Scrolls ...?

RELIGION
1117. ► Which Biblical Book involves the delivery of the Jewish people from slavery, their acceptance of the Covenant and their receiving the Law...?

HISTORY
1118. ► The Jews of Berlin formally dedicated their first synagogue in this century?

LANGUAGE **1119.** ► What is the *Kol Yisroel*?

GEOGRAPHY **1120.** ► What is ironic about the misnomers Dead Sea and Sea of Galilee...?

(Answers next page.)

ANSWERS

CURRENT EVENTS **1113.** ► **The exchange of 1,150 imprisoned Arab terrorists for three Israeli soldiers held in Lebanon. The argument used is: since convicted Arab terrorists are released so readily why shouldn't Israeli underground members receive similar consideration.**

WOMEN **1114.** ► **Barbra Streisand.**

ARTS & CULTURE **1115.** ► **Rembrandt.**

PEOPLE **1116.** ► **Professor Yigael Yadin.**

RELIGION **1117.** ► **The Book of Exodus.**

HISTORY **1118.** ► **The Eighteenth (1712).**

LANGUAGE **1119.** ► **The Israel radio service.**

GEOGRAPHY **1120.** ► **The Dead Sea is actually a large salt water lake and the Sea of Galilee is really a large fresh water lake.**

CURRENT
EVENTS

1121. ► Even though the area in question is only a few thousand square yards, Taba is important to Israel and Egypt because . . . ?

WOMEN

1122. ► This Jewish American writer is generally considered America's foremost female intellectual . . . ?

ARTS &
CULTURE

1123. ► He is sometimes referred to as the "Jewish Mark Twain" . . . ?

PEOPLE

1124. ► This prominent American Reform Jewish leader purposely kept the news of the Holocaust hidden from American Jewry for many months . . . ?

RELIGION

1125. ► Jewish religious law requires that a husband write and deliver a bill of divorce to his wife in order for the marriage to be terminated. A Jewish divorce is called . . . ?

HISTORY

1126. ► What position did Moshe Dayan hold in the Israeli governments of Moshe Sharett and David Ben-Gurion?

LANGUAGE

1127. ► What does the name *Abraham* mean?

GEOGRAPHY

1128. ► Haifa is in this direction from Tel Aviv . . . ?

(Answers next page.)

ANSWERS

CURRENT EVENTS 1121. ▶ It is valuable waterfront land on which Israeli developers have spent tens of millions of dollars developing resort hotels.

WOMEN 1122. ▶ Susan Sontag.

ARTS & CULTURE 1123. ▶ Sholom Aleichem.

PEOPLE 1124. ▶ Rabbi Stephen S. Wise. (He was asked by the U.S. government to suppress the news he had heard from the World Jewish Congress until it could be verified by the U.S. State Department.)

RELIGION 1125. ▶ A "get."

HISTORY 1126. ▶ Commander-in-Chief.

LANGUAGE 1127. ▶ Father of many.

GEOGRAPHY 1128. ▶ North.

Trivia Judaica -   QUESTIONS

CURRENT EVENTS   1129. ► The controversial war in Lebanon cost Israel how many lives...?

WOMEN   1130. ► *A Spy for Freedom*, a book by Irene Gunther and Ida Cohen, is the true story of this Jewish heroine...?

ARTS & CULTURE   1131. ► *Hena Matov, Shalom Alaychem, David Melech* and *Havanegelah* are all Jewish...?

PEOPLE   1132. ► This Zionist leader used the pen name *Altalena*...?

RELIGION   1133. ► Jewish law forbids the drinking of this liquid...?

HISTORY   1134. ► This British statesman said on February 8, 1920: "If there should be a Jewish State under the protection of the British Crown...an event will have occured in the history of the world which would...be beneficial, and would be especially in harmony with the truest interests of the British Empire...?

LANGUAGE   1135. ► The uncomplimentary term "Safe Jew" refers to this type of Jewish person?

GEOGRAPHY   1136. ► The Simon Wiesenthal Center for Holocaust Studies is located in...?

283   (Answers next page.)

ANSWERS

CURRENT EVENTS   1137. ► Approximately how many Ethiopian Jews escaped to Israel and how many still remain in Ethiopia . . . ?

WOMEN   1138. ► What is the name of the American movie about the life of Golda Meir and who played Golda . . . ?

ARTS & CULTURE   1139. ► Eliezer Ben Yehuda was a noted scholar in this area of research . . . ?

PEOPLE   1140. ► Name two Jewish major league baseball players in the baseball Hall of Fame . . . ?

RELIGION   1141. ► What are inside *Tefillin*?

HISTORY   1142. ► He was born in the 10th Century with the name Sholmo Ben Isaac and became the most renowned Bible commentator . . . ?

LANGUAGE   1143. ► In Yiddish one who is *shluffedik* is . . . ?

GEOGRAPHY   1144. ► Napolean was defeated and Moshe Dayan imprisoned in this same city in Palestine . . . ?

        (Answers next page.)

ANSWERS

1137. ► Approximately 10,000 escaped to Israel and at least 8,000 are thought to still remain.

WOMEN 1138. ► "Golda," starring Ingrid Bergman.

ARTS &
CULTURE 1139. ► Language (Ben Yehuda's dictionary).

PEOPLE 1140. ► Hank Greenberg and Sandy Koufax.

RELIGION 1141. ► Quotations from Exodus and Deuteronomy that are hand lettered in Hebrew on a small piece of paper.

HISTORY 1142. ► History.

LANGUAGE 1143. ► Sleepy or dull.

GEOGRAPHY 1144. ► Acre.

CURRENT EVENTS **1145.** ► Knesset Minister Shilansky has introduced a bill calling for the deportation of the "Black Hebrews" because some have "turned to crime" and "have a state within a state in Dimona." Where are they originally from . . . ?

WOMEN **1146.** ► She wrote the Jewish bestseller: *How to Run a Traditional Jewish Household*?

ARTS & CULTURE **1147.** ► This Jewish author won the 1958 Nobel Prize in Literature . . . ?

PEOPLE **1148.** ► This American President said: "Americans agree that in Palestine shall be laid the foundations of a Jewish commonwealth" . . . ?

RELIGION **1149.** ► This Jewish sage was sometimes referred to as the "second Moses" . . . ?

HISTORY **1150.** ► What organization did David Raziel and Avraham Stern form in 1938 before the creation of Israel?

LANGUAGE **1151.** ► The Yiddish words *Chazzen, Chazzer* and *Chazzerai* translate into these English words?

GEOGRAPHY **1152.** ► Anne Frank lived in this city . . . ?

ANSWERS

CURRENT EVENTS **1145.** ► The United States. (There are approximately 1,500 black Americans residing in the Negev towns of Dimona, Arad, and Mitzpe Ramon.)

WOMEN **1146.** ► Blu Greenberg.

ARTS & CULTURE **1147.** ► Boris Leonidovich Pasternak.

PEOPLE **1148.** ► Woodrow Wilson.

RELIGION **1149.** ► Moses Maimonides.

HISTORY **1150.** ► The Irgun Zvie Leumi or National Military Organization. (They were in the Revisionist party.)

LANGUAGE **1151.** ► Cantor, pig, trash.

GEOGRAPHY **1152.** ► Amsterdam.

CURRENT EVENTS   **1153.** ► Israeli's internal security, considered among the best in the world, is still vulnerable to this threat which has plagued U.S., British and West German intelligence and security establishments...?

WOMEN   **1154.** ► This excerpt comes from what book: "Sunday, 14 June, 1942. On Friday, June 12th, I woke up at 6:00 and no wonder; it was my birthday"...?

ARTS & CULTURE   **1155.** ► This Israeli statesman wrote *From These Men: Seven Founders of the State of Israel*...?

PEOPLE   **1156.** ► Which rabbi persuaded Cromwell to allow the Jews to return to England?

RELIGION   **1157.** ► On this Jewish holiday it is customary to eat a dairy meal...?

HISTORY   **1158.** ► When Chaim Weizmann took office as Israel's first president, what was he forced to relinquish...?

LANGUAGE   **1159.** ► When one is *krank* he or she is...?

GEOGRAPHY   **1160.** ► This is the only Arab country where Jews enjoy full equality and the Jewish community has full recognition...?

ANSWERS

1153. ► **Penetration of their military, political and intelligence establishments by the Soviet KGB.**

WOMEN **1154.** ► **From "Anne Frank: The Diary of a Young Girl."**

ARTS & CULTURE **1155.** ► **Shimon Peres.**

PEOPLE **1156.** ► **Rabbi Menasseh Ben Israel.**

RELIGION **1157.** ► **"Shavuos."**

HISTORY **1158.** ► **His British citizenship.**

LANGUAGE **1159.** ► **Ill.**

GEOGRAPHY **1160.** ► **Morocco. (King Hassan II is only anti-Semitic in his rhetoric.)**

CURRENT
EVENTS   **1161.** ▶ These three Mideast Nations seem to be in a competition to be Israel's worst enemy...?

WOMEN   **1162.** ▶ This Jewish American author, active in Ethiopian Jewish affairs, wrote the first children's book about Ethiopian Jews: *Falasha No More: An Ethiopian Jewish Child Comes Home*...?

ARTS &
CULTURE   **1163.** ▶ Jewish publisher Bennett Cerf, founded this major U.S. publishing firm...?

PEOPLE   **1164.** ▶ This Jewish leader founded the American Jewish Congress...?

RELIGION   **1165.** ▶ This Talmudic figure is referred to as the "Jewish Rip Van Winkle" because he slept for 700 years...?

HISTORY   **1166.** ▶ On Nov. 30th 1947, what was the Syrian Delegate to the UN referring to when he made this speech stating: "Arabs and Moslems throughout the world will obstruct it, and all Asia with its thousand million people will oppose it"?

LANGUAGE   **1167.** ▶ The day is_____, the task is _____? The missing words are ...?

GEOGRAPHY   **1168.** ▶ Raoul Wallenberg rescued tens of thousands of Jews mostly from this nation...?

ANSWERS

CURRENT EVENTS   **1161.** ► **Iran, Libya and Syria.**

WOMEN   **1162.** ► **Arlene Kushner.**

ARTS & CULTURE   **1163.** ► **Random House.**

PEOPLE   **1164.** ► **Stephen S. Wise.**

RELIGION   **1165.** ► **Honi ha Meagel.**

HISTORY   **1166.** ► **The U.N. Partition Plan of Palestine. (This speech occurred the day after the UN announcement.)**

LANGUAGE   **1167.** ► **Short, great.**

GEOGRAPHY   **1168.** ► **Hungary.**

CURRENT EVENTS **1169.** ► Some speculate that the recent change in Israel's hardline approach on this issue encouraged the 1985 Athens Airport hijacking and subsequent hostage crisis...?

WOMEN **1170.** ► What type of performing artist is Israel's Yaffa Yarkoni?

ARTS & CULTURE **1171.** ► Describe the symbols found on the Seal of Jerusalem?

PEOPLE **1172.** ► This Jewish intellectual encouraged German Jews to leave the ghettos and introduced them to German secular life ...?

RELIGION **1173.** ► The Jewish calendar differs from most other calendars because it is based on ...?

HISTORY **1174.** ► What were the names of the divided Jewish kingdoms of Biblical times?

LANGUAGE **1175.** ► How many letters are there in the Hebrew alphabet?

GEOGRAPHY **1176.** ► The *Golem* legend orginated in this East European city...?

(Answers next page.)

ANSWERS

CURRENT EVENTS **1169.** ► Israel's policy never to negotiate with terrorists was weakened when 1,150 Arab terrorists were exchanged for three Israeli soldiers.

WOMEN **1170.** ► A leading folk and pop singer.

ARTS & CULTURE **1171.** ► The Lion (of Judea) and olive branches, on the background of a wall.

PEOPLE **1172.** ► Moses Mendelssohn.

RELIGION **1173.** ► The lunar cycle rather than the sun's cycle.

HISTORY **1174.** ► The kingdom of Judah and The Kingdom of Israel.

LANGUAGE **1175.** ► 22.

GEOGRAPHY **1176.** ► Prague.

CURRENT
EVENTS

1177. ► The second most controversial plat-
form of Knesset member Meir Kahane
does not affect Arabs but is of concern
to the world Jewish community...?

WOMEN

1178. ► What is the name of the first and only
Jewish wife of this often married and
highly acclaimed Jewish bestselling
author...?

ARTS &
CULTURE

1179. ► Sholom Aleichem is the pen name of
this great Jewish writer...?

PEOPLE

1180. ► The statement, "Illegal immigration
should be the national sport of the
Jews" is credited to which great Jew?

RELIGION

1181. ► For a fish to be kosher it must have
these two characteristics...?

HISTORY

1182. ► What was the purpose of the "Wood-
head Commission," formed in 1938 by
the British government?

LANGUAGE

1183. ► The English translation of the Israeli
organization known as *Zahal* is...?

GEOGRAPHY

1184. ► The Suez Canal connects these two
seas...?

(Answers next page.)

ANSWERS

1177. ► The controversial definition of who is and who is not a Jew. Kahane has his own ideas about this, which if put into practice would not include substantial numbers of people who currently believe that they are Jews.

1178. ► Dr. Beatrice Silverman, Norman Mailer's first wife.

1179. ► Shlomo Rabinowitz.

1180. ► Vladimir Ze'ev Jabotinsky, (in response to the British quotas on Jews entering Palestine in the late 1930s).

1181. ► Fins and scales.

1182. ► To examine the proposed Palestine partition plans. (These were proposed by the Peel Commission, the Jewish Agency, and others.)

1183. ► Israel Defense Forces.

1184. ► The Red Sea and Mediterranean.

CURRENT
EVENTS   1185. ▶ Over the last few year, American combat aircraft fought planes of this Arab nation over the Gulf of Sidra...?

WOMEN   1186. ▶ Mrs. Miriam Groft conducted such an intense, persistent and personal campaign in Israel that many credited her with being responsible for the emotional pressure on the government that finally resulted in this controversial move...?

ARTS &
CULTURE   1187. ▶ This Jewish nightclub performer and popular singer was originally named Sidney Liebowitz...?

PEOPLE   1188. ▶ This Spanish poet was considered the greatest Jewish poet of the Middle Ages...?

RELIGION   1189. ▶ The Hebrew word for *Torah* is...?

HISTORY   1190. ▶ What does the HIAS organization stand for—and why was it formed?

LANGUAGE   1191. ▶ The less than complimentary Yiddish term *Plosher* refers to one who is?

GEOGRAPHY   1192. ▶ Jerusalem was built on how many hills...?

ANSWERS

CURRENT EVENTS **1185.** ► Libya. (American fighters shot down the Libyan planes when they approached a U.S. aircraft carrier.)

WOMEN **1186.** ► The exchange of three Israeli soldiers for 1,150 Arab terrorists. (Her son was one of the three soldiers.)

ARTS & CULTURE **1187.** ► Steve Lawrence.

PEOPLE **1188.** ► Yehudah Halevi.

RELIGION **1189.** ► "Chumash."

HISTORY **1190.** ► The Hebrew Sheltering and Immigrant Aid Society—a Jewish group organized to protect Jewish immigrants (established in 1887 in the U.S., it is still in existence today).

LANGUAGE **1191.** ► A gossip.

GEOGRAPHY **1192.** ► Seven.

CURRENT EVENTS   **1193.** ► This highly visible U.S. clergyman said: "The idea that religion and politics don't mix was invented by the devil to keep Christians from running their own country" and "we need an old-fashioned, God-honoring, Christ-exalted revival to turn America back to God...?"

WOMEN   **1194.** ► This female Jewish author wrote the *Jewish Kid's Catalog*?

ARTS & CULTURE   **1195.** ► Why does Michelangelo's statue of Moses depict him with two horns protruding from his head?

PEOPLE   **1196.** ► He was the commander of the Entebbe raid and was killed in action...?

RELIGION   **1197.** ► Name the two Books of Moses where the Ten Commandments are found?

HISTORY   **1198.** ► The king of Egypt was given this title...?

LANGUAGE   **1199.** ► Petach Tikvah is a town in Israel. Its name means...?

GEOGRAPHY   **1200.** ► Israel's northern mountain range is called...?

ANSWERS

1193. ► Reverend Jerry Falwell.

WOMEN 1194. ► Chaya M. Burstein.

ARTS &
CULTURE 1195. ► When the Bible was translated into Latin in the second century the Hebrew verb "Karan" (radiant) was confused with the noun "Keren" (horn) hence came the incorrect Latin translation that the head of Moses was horned instead of radiant.

PEOPLE 1196. ► Jonathan Netanyahu. (His brother is the Israeli Ambassador to the U.N., Benjamin Netanyahu.)

RELIGION 1197. ► Exodus and Deuteronomy.

HISTORY 1198. ► Pharaoh.

LANGUAGE 1199. ► Mother of the colony.

GEOGRAPHY 1200. ► The Golan Heights.

Trivia Judaica.   QUESTIONS

CURRENT EVENTS
1201. ▶ General Ariel Sharon could not collect the 50 million dollars he sued *Time* for even though the jury found that the magazine did lie and unjustly accuse him of murder because. . . ?

WOMEN
1202. ▶ The life of this Jewish leader is described in the book *My Life*. . . ?

ARTS & CULTURE
1203. ▶ Yitzhak Pearlman, the great violinist, suffers from this physical handicap. . . ?

PEOPLE
1204. ▶ This former president of Hebrew University was criticized for widely urging the creation of a bi-national Arab-Jewish "Palestine" instead of a Jewish State. . . ?

RELIGION
1205. ▶ Which food must be eaten during a meal in order for *Birkat Hamazon*, the traditional grace after meals, to be recited?

HISTORY
1206. ▶ Israel is administered by this type of government. . . ?

LANGUAGE
1207. ▶ How can one explain the difference between a *shlemazel* and a *shlemiel*?

GEOGRAPHY
1208. ▶ In October 1985, how and where did the Israeli government put a "return address" on P.L.O. terrorist violence?

301   (Answers next page.)

ANSWERS

CURRENT EVENTS 1201. ► The jury found that Time magazine did not act out of malice in accusing General Sharon.

WOMEN 1202. ► Golda Meir.

ARTS & CULTURE 1203. ► Polio. (He was crippled at the age of four and walks with the aid of crutches.)

PEOPLE 1204. ► Judah P. Magnes.

RELIGION 1205. ► Bread.

HISTORY 1206. ► A parliamentary democracy.

LANGUAGE 1207. ► The "shlemiel" drops hot soup in the "shlemazel's" lap.

GEOGRAPHY 1208. ► By sending Israeli bombers on a long range 1500 mile mission to destroy P.L.O. headquarters in Tunisia—demonstrating to terrorists that they cannot hide from the reach of the Israeli government. (Israel claimed that Tunisia was partially responsible for the actions of this terrorist group based on their territory.)

 (Answers next page.)

CURRENT
EVENTS
1209. ► King Hassan II of Morocco signed a treaty of union with this Middle East nation—surprising the Western world...?

WOMEN
1210. ► Naomi Shemer is a well known Israeli, famous for these two skills...?

ARTS &
CULTURE
1211. ► This Jewish author won the 1976 Pulitzer Prize for fiction for his novel *Humboldt's Gift*...?

PEOPLE
1212. ► He was a pre-State of Israel major freedom fighter, known to his followers as "Yair"...?

RELIGION
1213. ► The phrase that follows the Biblical quote: "What doth the Lord require of thee" is...?

HISTORY
1214. ► Before which Jewish conference in the late 19th Century was the Jewish flag first displayed?

LANGUAGE
1215. ► In the 1920s, this *Jewish Daily Forward* cartoon character became so well known that his name became an adopted Yiddish expression...?

GEOGRAPHY
1216. ► Israel's highest mountain is...?

ANSWERS

1209. ► **Libya.**

1210. ► **Song writing and singing.**

1211. ► **Saul Bellow.**

1212. ► **Avraham Stern.**

1213. ► **". . . but to do justly and to love mercy and to walk humbly with thy God."**

1214. ► **At the First Zionist Conference (Basel, Switzerland, 1897).**

1215. ► **"Moishe Kapoyer" meaning, one who does the opposite of what you want, one who is contrary.**

1216. ► **Mount Meron.**

CURRENT
EVENTS

1217. ► The *Mastif* and *Scout* are the names of a sophisticated weapon that Israel is exporting. This weapon is . . . ?

WOMEN

1218. ► This famous Jewish American female photojournalist specialized in photographing bizarre, grotesque and unusual people . . . ?

ARTS &
CULTURE

1219. ► Which famous Jewish philosopher did Albert Einstein say most closely resembled his own concept of the nature of God . . . ?

PEOPLE

1220. ► The arch-terrorist known as "The Jackal" is high on Israel's most-wanted list. By what name is he more commonly known?

RELIGION

1221. ► This religion began in the East and was based upon the Jewish idea of one God, also called monotheism . . . ?

HISTORY

1222. ► In 629, these conquerors under the leadership of Heraclius reoccupied Palestine, restored the Cross to Jerusalem, and expelled the Jews . . . ?

LANGUAGE

1223. ► The Hebrew word *Yishuv* stands for . . . ?

GEOGRAPHY

1224. ► What is the lowest city in Israel?

ANSWERS

CURRENT EVENTS **1217.** ► **Drone aircraft used for pilotless reconnaissance missions.**

WOMEN **1218.** ► **Diane Arbus.**

ARTS & CULTURE **1219.** ► **Spinoza.**

PEOPLE **1220.** ► **Carlos.**

RELIGION **1221.** ► **Islam.**

HISTORY **1222.** ► **The Byzantines.**

LANGUAGE **1223.** ► **Communal settlement.**

GEOGRAPHY **1224.** ► **Tiberias. (It is 210 meters below sea level.)**

CURRENT
EVENTS   **1225.** ► This Israeli political party believes that Israel has a Biblical obligation to retain the West Bank territories···?

WOMEN   **1226.** ► This female Jewish author wrote *The Book of Modern Jewish Etiquette* and *Your Jewish Wedding*...?

ARTS &
CULTURE   **1227.** ► These famous institutions all share a creation of this Jewish artist: The Paris Opera House, the Vatican, the U.N., and Hadassah Medical Center...?

PEOPLE   **1228.** ► He has been referred to by his admirers as Israel's "General Patton"...?

RELIGION   **1229.** ► How many candles is a Jewish woman required to light just prior to the onset of the Sabbath?

HISTORY   **1230.** ► The Assyrians sent these Jewish groups into exile...?

LANGUAGE   **1231.** ► The Yiddish exclamation *Feh* translates into...?

GEOGRAPHY   **1232.** ► Israel's only major body of freshwater is called...?

ANSWERS

CURRENT EVENTS	**1225.** ►	**"Gush Emunim."**
WOMEN	**1226.** ►	**Helen Latner.**
ARTS & CULTURE	**1227.** ►	**Marc Chagall's stained glass windows.**
PEOPLE	**1228.** ►	**General Ariel "Arik" Sharon.**
RELIGION	**1229.** ►	**One for each member of her family.**
HISTORY	**1230.** ►	**The Ten Tribes of Israel.**
LANGUAGE	**1231.** ►	**Baloney! or Phooey!**
GEOGRAPHY	**1232.** ►	**The Sea of Galilee.**

CURRENT
EVENTS   **1233.** ► During the Yom Kippur War how close to Damascus did Israeli forces get (with 5 miles accuracy)...?

WOMEN   **1234.** ► This Jewish female poet originated the poem inscribed on the Statue of Liberty, that included these words: "Huddled masses yearning to breathe free"...?

ARTS &
CULTURE   **1235.** ► This Jewish author won the 1952 Pulitzer Prize for Fiction for his book *The Caine Mutiny*...?

PEOPLE   **1236.** ► This Jewish statesman won the Nobel Peace Prize in 1973...?

RELIGION   **1237.** ► God ordered Moses to construct this type of wooden chest as a repository for the two Tablets of the Law...?

HISTORY   **1238.** ► The Holocaust occured between these dark years...?

LANGUAGE   **1239.** ► The Yiddish descriptive term *Amhorets* refers to this type of a person...?

GEOGRAPHY **1240.** ► The legendary ancient king, Antiochus Epiphanes, was king of this nation...?

ANSWERS

1233. ► **25 miles.**

1234. ► **Emma Lazarus.**

1235. ► **Herman Wouk.**

1236. ► **Henry Kissinger.**

1237. ► **The Ark of the Covenant.**

1238. ► **1939 to 1945.**

1239. ► **One who is uneducated, illiterate and ignorant.**

1240. ► **Greece.**

CURRENT
EVENTS

1241. ► What does AIPAC stand for?

WOMEN

1242. ► Brenda Patimkin is the Jewish heroine of this well-known novel...?

ARTS &
CULTURE

1243. ► This Jewish intellectual wrote *Making It* and is the editor of a monthly Jewish magazine...?

PEOPLE

1244. ► The great Jewish writer I.L. Peretz was born in this country and his initials stand for...?

RELIGION

1245. ► In Longfellow's *Psalm of Life* this famous sentence from the Book of Genesis which refers to dust and death —is quoted...?

HISTORY

1246. ► In an attempt to appease the world Jewish community, what other memorial to victims of the Holocaust did President Reagan briefly visit after his controversial stop at the German military cemetery at Bitburg...?

LANGUAGE

1248. ► Yiddish expression *Fartumelt* refers to one who is...?

GEOGRAPHY

1248. ► According to Jewish legend wise men are associated with this town...?

ANSWERS

1241. ► American-Israeli Political Action Committee (Israel's principal lobby in Washington, D.C.).

1242. ► "Goodbye Columbus" (by Philip Roth).

1243. ► Norman Podhoretz (editor of "Commentary").

1244. ► Poland, Itzhak Leib Peretz. (His descendent is the publisher of "The New Republic," Martin Peretz.)

1245. ► "For dust thou art and unto dust thou shalt return."

1246. ► The Bergen-Belsen death camp.

1247. ► Confused and disoriented.

1248. ► Chelm. (The wise men of Chelm.)

CURRENT EVENTS

1249. ► Before the 1984 Presidential election, this candidate said in a speech: "If Israel is ever forced to walk out of the U.N., the United States and Israel will walk out together?

WOMEN

1250. ► She was the youngest woman ever to serve in the U.S. Congress...?

ARTS & CULTURE

1251. ► *Rabbi Ben Ezra* was a poem written by this famous non-Jewish poet...?

PEOPLE

1252. ► Josephus was not only a talented Jewish general, but also renowned as...?

RELIGION

1253. ► He first called the Jews "The People of the Book"...?

HISTORY

1254. ► Name the three signers of the March 27th, 1979 Egyptian-Israeli Peace Treaty...?

LANGUAGE

1255. ► The Yiddish term *Metsieh* refers to...?

GEOGRAPHY

1256. ► This is the world's most famous memorial to the victims of the Holocaust ...?

ANSWERS

1249. ► President Ronald Reagan. (From an address at Temple Hillel, Long Island, N.Y., October 26, 1984.)

WOMEN **1250.** ► Elizabeth Holtzman (currently the district attorney for Brooklyn, New York).

ARTS & CULTURE **1251.** ► Robert Browning.

PEOPLE **1252.** ► A historian.

RELIGION **1253.** ► Mohammed.

HISTORY **1254.** ► Jimmy Carter, Menachem Begin, Anwar Sadat.

LANGUAGE **1255.** ► A real prize or a great discovery. (It is sometimes used sarcastically.)

GEOGRAPHY **1256.** ► Yad Vashem, located in Jerusalem.

CURRENT
EVENTS   1257. ▶ Israel has three major intelligence gathering organizations—one is similar to the CIA; another is equivalent to the FBI, the last branch deals with . . . ?

WOMEN   1258. ▶ The daughter of a wealthy assimilated family, Emma Lazarus was not of German Jewish origin, rather she was . . . ?

ARTS &
CULTURE   1259. ▶ This Jewish author wrote *Saturday the Rabbi Went Hungry, Sunday The Rabbi Stayed Home. Monday the Rabbi took off*, etc, etc . . . ?

PEOPLE   1260. ▶ At the age of thirty, he was David Ben-Gurion's chief aide; later he became Minister of Defense and then Prime Minister . . . ?

RELIGION   1261. ▶ In the Bible what famous line contrasts bread with life and people?

HISTORY   1262. ▶ Masada fell in this year . . . ?

LANGUAGE   1263. ▶ This Jewish delicacy is made from grated potatoes fried in oil . . . ?

GEOGRAPHY   1264. ▶ Israel is on this continent . . . ?

       (Answers next page.)

ANSWERS

CURRENT EVENTS 1257. ► Military Intelligence, (it handles the gathering of information on Arab armies; providing daily analyses of political developments for government leaders).

WOMEN 1258. ► Sephardic.

ARTS & CULTURE 1259. ► Harry Kemelman.

PEOPLE 1260. ► Shimon Peres.

RELIGION 1261. ► "Man doth not live by bread alone," (Deuteronomy).

HISTORY 1262. ► 73 C.E.

LANGUAGE 1263. ► "Latkes."

GEOGRAPHY 1264. ► Asia.

CURRENT EVENTS   1265. ▶ For what specific reason did the U.S. Navy recently lease a squadron of Israeli Kifir fighter jets?

WOMEN   1266. ▶ She is remembered not only for her contributions to the field of social service but also as the famous "Anna O" whose case history led Freud to his discovery of the unconscious...?

ARTS & CULTURE   1267. ▶ Jewish actor, Walter Matthau, first played the stage role that was later popularized on T.V. by Jewish actor Jack Klugman...?

PEOPLE   1268. ▶ He was the first American president to visit Israel while in office...?

RELIGION   1269. ▶ Drinking, generally frowned upon by Jews, is actually encouraged on this holiday...?

HISTORY   1270. ▶ What was another name for "Etzel"?

LANGUAGE   1271. ▶ The "J" sound in English translates to what spoken sound in Hebrew?

GEOGRAPHY   1272. ▶ This city was under siege for a long time during Israel's War of Independence ...?

(Answers next page.)

ANSWERS

1265. ► They are best at simulating Soviet jets in the tactical training of U.S. pilots. (Their configuration and performance are similar to Soviet Migs.)

1266. ► Bertha Pappenheim.

1267. ► Oscar Madison ("The Odd Couple").

1268. ► Richard M. Nixon.

1269. ► Purim.

1270. ► The Irgun Zvei Leumi (National Military Organization).

1271. ► The "Y" sound. (Joseph is Yosef in Hebrew.)

1272. ► Jerusalem.

CURRENT
EVENTS   **1273.** ► In this Arab nation, American military planes have refueling rights, U.S. nuclear-powered vessels have access and the Voice of America is permitted to broadcast its programs....?

WOMEN   **1274.** ► The oldest Jewish service organization, founded in 1843 did not grant women complete representation and full delegate status until 1950...?

ARTS &
CULTURE   **1275.** ► William Styron wrote this novel about the Holocaust that became a movie...?

PEOPLE   **1276.** ► Levi Yitzhak of Berdichev had many books written about him because he was renowned as...?

RELIGION   **1277.** ► These three Jewish leaders were all prominent in this movement of Judaism: Max Lilienthal, David Einhorn and Samuel Hirsch...?

HISTORY   **1278.** ► When Caliph Omar conquered the Holy Land in 636 C.E. what was the most significant action that he took concerning the Jewish people?

LANGUAGE   **1279.** ► The common descriptive Yiddish term *Meeskeit* means...?

GEOGRAPHY   **1280.** ► The Jewish "Pale of Settlement" was located in...?

ANSWERS

1273. ► Morocco.

1274. ► "B'nai B'rith."

1275. ► "Sophie's Choice."

1276. ► A classical rabbi and great Jewish leader.

1277. ► The American Reform Movement.

1278. ► He opened Jerusalem to Jewish settlement. (This was the first time since the Roman conquest in 70 C.E. that the Jewish people were actually welcomed in Jerusalem and not simply tolerated.)

1279. ► A physically ugly person or thing.

1280. ► The Ukraine.

CURRENT
EVENTS

1281. ▶ In a New York synagogue, ten days before the presidential election, this presidential candidate claimed that, "American marines were sent to Lebanon to prevent another Holocaust of Jews"...?

WOMEN

1282. ▶ She played Golda Meir in the Broadway show *Golda*...?

ARTS &
CULTURE

1283. ▶ The Israeli Bialik Prize is awarded to ...?

PEOPLE

1284. ▶ When in a bad mood, this American general referred to President Franklin D. Roosevelt as "Rosenfeld" and would refer to President Truman as "That Jew in the White House"...?

RELIGION

1285. ▶ At what angle is a *mezuzah* supposed to be tilted on the doorpost of a Jewish home?

HISTORY

1286. ▶ Early settlers in Palestine were afflicted with this disease more than any other...?

LANGUAGE

1287. ▶ The Hebrew language study program that intensively teaches non-speakers is known as...?

GEOGRAPHY

1288. ▶ The ancient name for the Land of Israel was...?

ANSWERS

1281. ▶ Ronald Reagan. (The Union of American Hebrew Congregations assailed these comments as being "false and grossly offensive." Reagan may have meant to say that marines were sent to oversee the evacuation of the PLO front from Beirut.)

1282. ▶ Ann Bancroft.

1283. ▶ Writers.

1284. ▶ Gen. Douglas MacArthur (according to his personal security officer, Major Faubion Bowers).

1285. ▶ The top should be tilting in toward the home.

1286. ▶ Malaria (from the insects living in the numerous swamps throughout the land of pre-State Israel).

1287. ▶ "Ulpan" (the Ulpan system of the Jewish Agency).

1288. ▶ Canaan.

CURRENT
EVENTS
1289. ► This non-Jewish U.S. senator sponsored a Congressional resolution which condemned the passage, 10 years ago, of the infamous resolution that branded Zionism as racism...?

WOMEN
1290. ► This wealthy Philadelphia-born Jewish woman refused to intermarry and served as the model for the gentle Jewess Rebecca in Sir Walter Scott's novel *Ivanhoe*...?

ARTS &
CULTURE
1291. ► The *B'nai B'rith* publishes a magazine called...?

PEOPLE
1292. ► France's most famous Jewish automobile maker is...?

RELIGION
1293. ► The most villified concept in the *Torah*, often denounced as barbaric, is this law that prevents punishment in excess of the crime committed...?

HISTORY
1294. ► When the noted Jewish scholar, Rambam, settled in Palestine in 1267, and set up a synogogue, this group was in power in the area...?

LANGUAGE
1295. ► The Yiddish word *Kopvaitik* means?

GEOGRAPHY
1296. ► This country is east of Israel...?

 (Answers next page.)

ANSWERS

CURRENT EVENTS   **1289.** ► **Senator Alfonse D'Amato.**

WOMEN   **1290.** ► **Rebecca Gratz.**

ARTS & CULTURE   **1291.** ► **The "Jewish Monthly."**

PEOPLE   **1292.** ► **Citroen, named after its founder Andre Citroen.**

RELIGION   **1293.** ► **"An eye for an eye, a tooth for a tooth."**

HISTORY   **1294.** ► **The Christian Crusaders.**

LANGUAGE   **1295.** ► **Headache.**

GEOGRAPHY   **1296.** ► **Jordan.**

CURRENT
EVENTS   **1297.** ► Who was the Israeli government attempting to restrain by passing legislation that would prohibit racist demaguery by politicians and public servants?

WOMEN   **1298.** ► This Jewish writer was known as "the supreme poetess of Jewish suffering" and "a poet of the people"...?

ARTS &
CULTURE   **1299.** ► This Israeli author wrote *The Bridal Canopy* and *The Book of Tales*...?

PEOPLE   **1300.** ► This Jewish entrepreneur, a regular in the Forbes 400, arranges large-scale wheat deals with the Soviet Union and owns one of the largest privately-held commodity trading firms in the world ...?

RELIGION   **1301.** ► What is the difference between Judaism and asceticism...?

HISTORY   **1302.** ► He was the first Jew to be elected to the United States Senate, representing Louisiana, he also served as Secretary of State in the government of the Confederacy...?

LANGUAGE   **1303.** ► The much used Yiddish exclamation, *kinah hora* means?

GEOGRAPHY   **1304.** ► This city has more synagogues than any other city in the world...?

ANSWERS

<table>
<tr><td>CURRENT EVENTS</td><td>1297.</td><td>► Rabbi Meir Kahane of Israel's Kach Party.</td></tr>
<tr><td>WOMEN</td><td>1298.</td><td>► Emma Lazarus.</td></tr>
<tr><td>ARTS & CULTURE</td><td>1299.</td><td>► S.Y. Agnon.</td></tr>
<tr><td>PEOPLE</td><td>1300.</td><td>► Michel Fribourg(owner of the Continental Grain Company).</td></tr>
<tr><td>RELIGION</td><td>1301.</td><td>► Ascetism advocates self-denial as an act of religious devotion while Judaism emphasizes tolerance and participation in a vibrant community life.</td></tr>
<tr><td>HISTORY</td><td>1302.</td><td>► Judah Benjamin.</td></tr>
<tr><td>LANGUAGE</td><td>1303.</td><td>► Knock on wood or spare us the evil eye!</td></tr>
<tr><td>GEOGRAPHY</td><td>1304.</td><td>► New York City.</td></tr>
</table>

CURRENT EVENTS   **1305.** ► This Mideast leader offers Shiite terrorists safe havens and by doing so encourages them. He controls events in Lebanon by keeping warring factions dependent on him for arms and money . . . ?

WOMEN   **1306.** ► Historically barred from active roles in worship, women established these organizations as a means of participating in the life of the synagogue . . . ?

ARTS & CULTURE   **1307.** ► This anti-Semitic forgery gained widespread credence in the early part of the 20th Century. It played a great part in Nazi propaganda . . . ?

PEOPLE   **1308.** ► This chemical in the periodic table is named in honor of a great Jewish scientist . . . ?

RELIGION   **1309.** ► What is the *Mikra*?

HISTORY   **1310.** ► What was the Jewish and Arab reaction to the recommendations of the "Peel Commission," made in July 1937?

LANGUAGE   **1311.** ► A foreign substance or demon that inhabits a living person is known as . . . ?

GEOGRAPHY   **1312.** ► The Hebrew word for beautiful is the same as the name of this port city . . . ?

     (Answers next page.)

ANSWERS

CURRENT EVENTS
1313. ► Abie Nathan was famous for his special ship that traveled around the world. What activity did the ship engage in to raise revenues?

WOMEN
1314. ► These four categories of women are exempt from military service in Israel...?

ARTS & CULTURE
1315. ► This Jewish voice over performer is responsible for the sounds behind a popular rabbit, pig and duck...?

PEOPLE
1316. ► This Russian leader killed massive numbers of Jews in the 1940's and 1950's, charging them with the crime of "Zionism"...?

RELIGION
1317. ► In the Book of Leviticus, the "Golden Rule" refers to this...?

HISTORY
1318. ► During the reign of Louis the 14th, with the signing of this formal treaty, Jews were allowed to re-enter France...?

LANGUAGE
1319. ► The word *Sephardic* literally means...?

GEOGRAPHY
1320. ► While climbing to the top of Masada one must walk on this path...?

ANSWERS

1313. ► It broadcast "The Voice of Peace" radio show, urging tolerance between Arabs and Jews and sold advertising spots on its air waves.

WOMEN 1314. ► Married women, women who have children, pregnant women, and women who claim religious belief as a basis for exemption.

ARTS &
CULTURE 1315. ► Mel Blanc (alias Bugs Bunny, Daffy Duck, and Porky the Pig).

PEOPLE 1316. ► Joseph Stalin.

RELIGION 1317. ► "Love Thy Neighbor."

HISTORY 1318. ► The Treaty of Westphalia (1648).

LANGUAGE 1319. ► One from Spain (or "Spharad" in Hebrew).

GEOGRAPHY 1320. ► The Snake Path.

CURRENT
EVENTS   1321. ► During the recent Shiite terrorist hijacking drama at Athens airport, this Arab dictator cynically manipulated the U.S. and rehabilitated his desperado image to the world by positioning himself as a statesman and conciliator . . . ?

WOMEN   1322. ► The wife of a rabbi is known as a . . . ?

ARTS &
CULTURE   1323. ► This renowned Jewish lyricist collaborated with Richard Rodgers to produce such smash musicals as *Babes in Arms* and *Pal Joey* . . . ?

PEOPLE   1324. ► This Jewish entrepreneur owns a company bearing his name that sells and manufactures hair, health and beauty items . . . ?

RELIGION   1325. ► Identify two tenets of Christianity that have their origins in Jewish beliefs . . . ?

HISTORY   1326. ► What do these places and dates have in common: England in 1290; France in 1306; Spain in 1492; and Austria, in 1670?

LANGUAGE   1327. ► The Yiddish descriptive term *farpotshket* means . . . ?

GEOGRAPHY   1328. ► This Israeli city is known as the "Gateway to the Negev" . . . ?

ANSWERS

1321. ► Syria's President Assad. (He finances and controls the terrorist group with whom he supposedly "helped" negotiate a settlement.)

1322. ► "Rebbetzin" (an affectionate term).

1323. ► Lorenz Hart.

1324. ► Vidal Sassoon.

1325. ► Any two of these: The Kingdom of God, the Messiah, and the Holy Spirit.

1326. ► The Jewish populations of these European cities were expelled.

1327. ► Messed up or difficult.

1328. ► Beersheba.

CURRENT
EVENTS

1329. ▶ What is the position of the *Likud* Party on Jewish settlements in the West Bank territories?

WOMEN

1330. ▶ Born in Berlin, the verse of this poet dealt with Holocaust themes. In 1966, together with S.Y. Agnon, she was awarded the Nobel Prize for Literature . . .?

ARTS &
CULTURE

1331. ▶ This play with a Jewish theme, was the longest running Broadway production of its era . . .?

PEOPLE

1332. ▶ During a 1974 visit to a Palestinian refugee camp, this American athlete publicly stated: "In my name and the name of all Muslims in America, I declare support for the Palestinian struggle to liberate their homeland and oust the Zionist invaders" . . .?

RELIGION

1333. ▶ What was the reasoning behind the ancient Hebrews' disgust with idolatrous religions?

HISTORY

1334. ▶ In 1953, this Jewish politician was elected prime minister of France . . .?

LANGUAGE

1335. ▶ What does the Hebrew word *Histadrut* translate to in English?

GEOGRAPHY

1336. ▶ These two countries separate Israel and Iran . . .?

(Answers next page.)

ANSWERS

CURRENT EVENTS 1329. ▶ Immediate expansion of the Israeli presence.

WOMEN 1330. ▶ Nelly Sachs.

ARTS & CULTURE 1331. ▶ "Fiddler on The Roof."

PEOPLE 1332. ▶ Muhammed Ali. (He publicly reiterated this position on several occasions over the years.)

RELIGION 1333. ▶ They viewed idolatry as linked to immoral practices and behavior.

HISTORY 1334. ▶ Rene Mayer.

LANGUAGE 1335. ▶ Organization. (Histadrut was founded in 1921 and is known as the General Federation of Jewish Labor.)

GEOGRAPHY 1336. ▶ Iraq and Jordan.

CURRENT
EVENTS

1337. ► Colonel Qadaffi's aid to rebels in the Sudan caused the overthrow of President Nimeiry and the installation of this new ruler . . . ?

WOMEN

1338. ► Orthodox rabbis exempt women from all time-bound commandments such as reciting the *Shema* and putting on *tefillin* because . . . ?

ARTS &
CULTURE

1339. ► The largest American collection of Jewish art works, literature and ceremonial objects are on display at . . . ?

PEOPLE

1340. ► What did Victor Kugler do to distinguish himself as a "righteous gentile" . . . ?

RELIGION

1341. ► This well known line from the *Talmud* is the basis for the Jewish imperative to be clean . . . ?

HISTORY

1342. ► What was King Solomon's main source of wealth?

LANGUAGE

1343. ► The Yiddish adjective *oysgamitched* refers to one who is . . . ?

GEOGRAPHY

1344. ► In 1776, Benjamin Franklin, Thomas Jefferson and John Adams, in equating the American Revolution with the situation of the ancient Jews, suggested a new government seal featuring Moses, the Israelites, Pharaoh's army and a pillar of fire. Who was the Israelite's equivalent to the King of England and where did he come from?

ANSWERS

1337. ► Gen. Abdel Dahab. (He claims his ties with Libya will not weaken U.S.-Sudanese relations.)

1338. ► They need sufficient time to supervise their families and care for their homes.

1339. ► The Hebrew Union College in Cincinnati, Ohio.

1340. ► He hid the family of Anne Frank for 25 months.

1341. ► "Cleanliness is next to Godliness."

1342. ► His merchant navy. (He also did well because of the harbor he constructed on the Red Sea and the smelting furnaces for copper and iron he developed in the Negev.)

1343. ► All worn out.

1344. ► The Pharaoh of Egypt.

CURRENT EVENTS   **1345.** ► These words of Rabbi Joseph B. Solovei-tchik: "When Jewish blood is shed by the enemy, there is no separation between the blood of secularists and religionists" —are especially important today because of the heightened tensions between these leading forces in the American Jewish community . . . ?

WOMEN   **1346.** ► The section of the *Talmud* entitled *Nashim* means . . . ?

ARTS & CULTURE   **1347.** ► This great Yiddish star was considered the Charlie Chaplin of the Jewish theater . . . ?

PEOPLE   **1348.** ► In 1974, commenting on Jewish influence in the U.S., this American general said: "Its so strong you wouldn't believe it . . . . They own large banks in this country, the newspapers . . . ?

RELIGION   **1349.** ► This rabbi founded the first "Liberal" Congregation in England . . . ?

HISTORY   **1350.** ► The Emir Feisal, a powerful Bedouin sheik, had strong views about the Balfour Doctrine and the creation of Israel. These views tilted toward . . . ?

LANGUAGE   **1351.** ► The derogatory Yiddish word *Farbisseneh* refers to one who is . . . ?

GEOGRAPHY   **1352.** ► In 1968, Israel began constuction of a fortified buffer zone called the "Bar Lev Line." What countries are separated by this boundary?

ANSWERS

QUESTIONS

CURRENT
EVENTS
1345. ► The Conservative and Reform movements lack of compatability with certain areas of Orthodox Jewish beliefs. (Anti-Semites treat all Jews equally as recorded history has demonstrated).

WOMEN
1346. ► Women.

ARTS &
CULTURE
1347. ► Menasha Skulnick.

PEOPLE
1348. ► Chairman of the Joint Chiefs of Staff, Gen. George S. Brown.

RELIGION
1349. ► Claude Montefiore.

HISTORY
1350. ► Support of the Balfour Doctrine and working peacefully together with the Jewish settlers without conflict (he stipulated that Arab residents would have full protection and rights).

LANGUAGE
1351. ► Bitter or angry.

GEOGRAPHY
1352. ► Egypt and Israel.

CURRENT
EVENTS

1353. ► This Latin American nation sponsored an International Day of Solidarity with the Palestinian People . . . ?

WOMEN

1354. ► This Jewish playwright authored *The Little Foxes, Toys in the Attic*, and *The Children's Hour* . . . ?

ARTS &
CULTURE

1355. ► This internationally acclaimed Israeli writer chronicles Israeli life in both fiction and journalistic sketches . . . ?

PEOPLE

1356. ► What was the reaction of Lord Moyne, Britain's Middle East Minister, to Adolph Eichmann's offer to trade 100,000 Jews for trucks, soap and coffee . . . ?

RELIGION

1357. ► The Shabbat between Rosh Hashanah and Yom Kippur is called . . . ?

HISTORY

1358. ► Between 1818 and the 1850s, the Jewish population of the United States jumped from barely 3,000 to (within 10% accuracy) . . . ?

LANGUAGE

1359. ► The Yiddish exclamation *ehmes!* means . . . ?

GEOGRAPHY

1360. ► Israel's northernmost town is . . . ?

ANSWERS

CURRENT EVENTS   1353. ▶ **Argentina. (On Nov. 29th, 1984 government officials participated in this meeting sponsored by the Argentine-Arab Foundation.)**

WOMEN   1354. ▶ **Lillian Hellman.**

ARTS & CULTURE   1355. ▶ **Amos Oz.**

PEOPLE   1356. ▶ **He turned down the offer, stating, "A hundred thousand Jews! What am I to do with them? Where am I to put them?"**

RELIGION   1357. ▶ **"Shabbat shuva" (the Sabbath of return).**

HISTORY   1358. ▶ **Approximately 150,000.**

LANGUAGE   1359 ▶ **Honestly! or Truly!**

GEOGRAPHY   1360. ▶ **Metula.**

CURRENT EVENTS

1361. ► This Israeli commission investigated the responsibility for the mass killings at Sabra and Shatilla...?

WOMEN

1362. ► She was buried in the martyrs' section of the Jewish Cemetery in Budapest. Later her body was moved to Israel where it was buried in the national military cemetery with highest military honors...?

ARTS & CULTURE

1363. ► What is the poet Naphtali Herz Imber (1856-1909) most famous for?

PEOPLE

1364. ► Archbishop Velerian Trife was deported from the U.S. because of his documented wartime activities in this fascist Rumanian organization that he led...?

RELIGION

1365. ► What is unusual about the timing of the *Rosh Hashanah* celebration?

HISTORY

1366. ► What organization did Avraham Stern form in 1940 Palestine that was later lead by Natan Friedman-Yellin?

LANGUAGE

1367. ► A *macher* is...?

GEOGRAPHY

1368. ► The ancient Jews in Egypt lived in this Biblical land...?

ANSWERS

1361. ► The Kahan Commission. (Yitzak Kahan was the judge who led the commission.)

WOMEN **1362.** ► Hannah Senesh.

ARTS &
CULTURE **1363.** ► He wrote the song "Hatikvah."

PEOPLE **1364.** ► The Iron Guard. They incited pogroms against the Jewish community of Bucharest in 1941, killing thousands.

RELIGION **1365.** ► That the New Year should begin in the seventh and not the first month.

HISTORY **1366.** ► The "Lechi" or Israel Freedom Fighters (a revisionist underground movement).

LANGUAGE **1367.** ► An organizer or an official. It is sometimes used affectionately such as "He is a big 'macher'."

GEOGRAPHY **1368.** ► Goshen.

CURRENT
EVENTS   **1369.** ▶ What gesture did former Canadian prime minister, Joe Clark, say he would make to Israel that the current prime minister, Brian Maloney, has refused to implement?

WOMEN   **1370.** ▶ The early women pioneers who left their comfortable middle-class homes in eastern Europe for Palestine were known in Hebrew as... ?

ARTS &
CULTURE   **1371.** ▶ The book *J'Accuse* —an exposé on France's anti-Semitic Dreyfus affair—was written by this non-Jew... ?

PEOPLE   **1372.** ▶ Noted playwright and screenwriter Ben Hecht's 1961 book *Perfidy* is controversial because it takes this extremely anti-establishment view of the Holocaust, stating... ?

RELIGION   **1373.** ▶ The main difference between the Jewish Priests and Prophets was... ?

HISTORY   **1374.** ▶ The laws that Russia enacted in May of 1882, which prohibited Jews from acquiring property except in certain areas called the Pale of Settlement, were know as the infamous... ?

LANGUAGE   **1375.** ▶ The affectionate Yiddish expression *Neshomeleh* means... ?

GEOGRAPHY   **1376.** ▶ The direction from Jerusalem to Tel Aviv is... ?

ANSWERS

1369. ► **Transfer Canada's Tel Aviv Embassy to Israel's official capital—Jerusalem. (Arab nations protested and the new prime minister backed down.)**

1370. ► **"Halutzot" (pioneers).**

1371. ► **Emile Zola.**

1372. ► **The Zionist establishment could have done much more to save Jews during the Holocaust. (He believed the establishment wanted more world sympathy and fewer Orthodox "Shtetl" Jews.)**

1373. ► **Priests had to abide by the customs and rituals of the Temple or a local synagogue, while Prophets were freelance-oriented and concerned more with the spirit of the religion than its formal ceremonies.**

1374. ► **May Laws (finally revoked in 1917).**

1375. ► **One who is a sweetheart.**

1376. ► **West.**

CURRENT
EVENTS
1377. ► What conflict do some people consider Israel's greatest misfortune since the inception of the Jewish State of Israel?"

WOMEN
1378. ► What form of dress is prohibited to traditional Orthodox women under any and all circumstances...?

ARTS &
CULTURE
1379. ► This legendary Jewish composer of popular music wrote over 100 stage shows and almost 1,000 songs, including the ever-popular hit *Ol' Man River*...?

PEOPLE
1380. ► In 1973 a prominent Republican politician was widely reported to have said: "These Jewboys are everywhere. You can't stop them."...?

RELIGION
1381. ► According to the Bible, what did God create on the 7th day...?

HISTORY
1382. ► The Spanish Inquisition refers specifically to...?

LANGUAGE
1383. ► The descriptive Yiddish term *Patshken* refers to one who is...?

GEOGRAPHY
1384. ► This famous Roman horse racing ruin is located in Caesarea and is referred to as...?

(Answers next page.)

ANSWERS

QUESTIONS

CURRENT EVENTS **1377.** ► The Lebanon War.

WOMEN **1378.** ► Sexually provocative fashion, such as very short skirts, bare legs and low-cut necklines.

ARTS & CULTURE **1379.** ► Jerome Kern.

PEOPLE **1380.** ► President Richard M. Nixon, in a taped conversation with John Dean.

RELIGION **1381.** ► Nothing. It was the Sabbath—a time to rest.

HISTORY **1382.** ► Religious courts to punish Jews for practicing their religion.

LANGUAGE **1383.** ► A lazy or half-hearted worker.

GEOGRAPHY **1384.** ► The Hippodrome.

CURRENT EVENTS

1385. ► What was the reaction of the Conservative movement's rabbis to the *Knesset* vote addressing the issue of who is and who is not a Jew, and the requirement that all conversions to Judaism be in accordance with strict Orthodox interpretation of religious law (*Halacha*)?

WOMEN

1386. ► According to the Old Testament, this woman, angered by her exile from the Garden of Eden, became a vengeful demon, tempting pious men to sexual desire...?

ARTS & CULTURE

1387. ► This Jewish songwriter donates all of his royalties from the song "God Bless America" to the Boy Scouts and Girl Scouts of America...?

PEOPLE

1388. ► Today, this man is a senior Israeli cabinet minister, but during the Six-Day War he was Israel's Chief of Staff...?

RELIGION

1389. ► What is the Chanukah *shamash*?

HISTORY

1390. ► From 1099 to 1291, this group controlled Jerusalem and mercilessly persecuted and killed the Jews of Palestine...?

LANGUAGE

1391. ► The Yiddish word *Balmeluhkeh* refers to one who is a...?

GEOGRAPHY

1392. ► The first Sephardic synagogue in the eastern hemisphere was founded on this island in 1732...?

(Answers next page.)

ANSWERS

1385. ► They decided to bar from their synagogues Knesset members who voted to further restrict the definition of who is a Jew. (This action was taken after a resolution had been adopted at the convention of Conservative rabbis.)

WOMEN 1386. ► Lilith.

ARTS &
CULTURE 1387. ► Irving Berlin.

PEOPLE 1388. ► Yitzak Rabin.

RELIGION 1389. ► The ninth candle on the "menorah" used to light the other candles. Literally, it means "servant."

HISTORY 1390. ► The Christian Crusaders

LANGUAGE 1391. ► Connoisseur (a sarcastic overtone is implied).

GEOGRAPHY 1392. ► Curacao.

CURRENT
EVENTS   **1393.** ► While several thousand Ethiopian Jews were stranded in the Sudan, a secret letter was drafted by the U.S. Senate and sent to President Reagan requesting that he intervene and assist these refugees get to Israel. How many senators signed the letter...?

WOMEN   **1394.** ► She wrote *Bloodshed, The Pagan Rabbi*, and *Trust*...?

ARTS &
CULTURE   **1395.** ► This Jewish singer was originally named Izzie Itzkowitz...?

PEOPLE   **1396.** ► In 1964, this Black leader said: "In America the Jews sap the very lifeblood of the so-called Negro to maintain the State of Israel, its armies, and its continued aggression...?

RELIGION   **1397.** ► This famous sentence in the Book of Job refers to the Lord and concerns both death and life...?

HISTORY   **1398.** ► This Temple, established in 1749, is the oldest surviving Reform Jewish congregation in the world and the first one built in the United States...?

LANGUAGE   **1399.** ► *Kunny-Lemel* refers to this type of behavior...?

GEOGRAPHY   **1400.** ► In 1940 legislation was introduced in Congress, and then voted down, that would have allowed Jewish refugees to settle in this part of the U.S....?

ANSWERS

1393. ▶ **The entire U.S. Senate. (There were actually 106 signatures— six Senators accidentally signed twice!)**

1394. ▶ **Cynthia Ozick.**

1395. ▶ **Eddie Cantor.**

1396. ▶ **Malcolm X.**

1397. ▶ **"The Lord giveth, and the Lord taketh away..."**

1398. ▶ **Beth Elohim, located in Charleston, South Carolina.**

1399. ▶ **Immature, clown-like or dumb.**

1400. ▶ **Alaska.**

CURRENT EVENTS

1401. ► In 1975, Simon Wiesenthal informed authorities of the whereabouts of Nazi war criminal Walter Kutschmann. The ADL recently gave this same information to a U.S. Senate committee. In what Latin American nation is Kutschmann living...?

WOMEN

1402. ► This Jewish woman was a Biblical judge...?

ARTS & CULTURE

1403. ► This Jewish comedian was born Alfred Schneider and later came to be known as The Outrageous...?

PEOPLE

1404. ► This Jewish American statesman and former editor of *The Nation* served as territorial governor of Alaska, and later became the first U.S. senator from that state...?

RELIGION

1405. ► Identify three major practices of Orthodox Judaism that differ from the Reform approach...?

HISTORY

1406. ► What was the Russian "Black Hundred?"

LANGUAGE

1407. ► This Yiddish food is made by frying crushed matzohs that are mixed together with eggs and milk. It is called...?

GEOGRAPHY

1408. ► These Israeli ruins are known as the "Castle of the Pilgrims...?"

ANSWERS

1401. ► Argentina. (He works for the Osram Electric Company, a West German firm based in Argentina.)

1402. ► Deborah.

1403. ► Lenny Bruce.

1404. ► Senator Ernest H. Gruening.

1405. ► The Orthodox: "Teffilin" are used by men during prayer. The sexes are separated while worshipping. The laws of "Kashrut" are observed. Married women are required to go to the "Mikvah." Men pray with a covered head.

1406. ► The group that directed the pogroms against the Jews under the orders of the Russian government.

1407. ► Matzah brie. (Serve either scrambled or in the form of a fried or baked pie.)

1408. ► "Atlit." (They are on the coast, just south of Mt. Carmel.)

CURRENT
EVENTS

1409. ► Where is the tiny controversial slice of land called Taba located?

WOMEN

1410. ► In 1912, Jewish feminist, Margaret Sanger, became the impetus behind this important movement...?

ARTS &
CULTURE

1411. ► In 1635, this legendary non-Jewish artist painted "Abraham's Sacrifice"...?

PEOPLE

1412. ► Rambam, Maimonides and Rabbi Moshe ben Maimon are all...?

RELIGION

1413. ► How did Reform Judaism change the length of observance of certain Holy Days?

HISTORY

1414. ► The *Palyam* conducted these type of operations for the *Palmach*...?

LANGUAGE

1415. ► The derogatory Yiddish term *bulven* refers to...?

GEOGRAPHY

1416. ► Which country was the most aggressive in provoking Israel prior to the 1967 Six-Day War?

ANSWERS

CURRENT
EVENTS   **1409.** ► Between Israel and Egypt in the north-eastern corner of the Sinai (both countries claim ownership of this area).

WOMEN   **1410.** ► Birth control (after a friend died of an abortion).

ARTS &
CULTURE   **1411.** ► Rembrandt.

PEOPLE   **1412.** ► Different names for the same famous person, most often referred to as Maimonides.

RELIGION   **1413.** ► They ended the second day of observance. (They believed that it was unnecessary since accurate calendars became available that were able to precisely identify the lunar based Jewish holidays. In early times, the second day was celebrated to be sure the holiday wasn't missed due to faulty lunar calendars.)

HISTORY   **1414.** ► Naval operations.

LANGUAGE   **1415.** ► A big oaf, lout, or idiot.

GEOGRAPHY   **1416.** ► Egypt. (Egyptian President Nasser led the other Arab states into this war.)

CURRENT
EVENTS   **1417.** ► What is unique and shocking about Israel's listing in the *1985 Encyclopedia Britannica Yearbook*?

WOMEN   **1418.** ► This Jewish writer immortalized the words in a poem: "A rose is a rose is a rose...?"

ARTS &
CULTURE   **1419.** ► The Black Jews of Ethiopia call themselves by what name?

PEOPLE   **1420.** ► How many different people have served as Prime Minister of the State of Israel?

RELIGION   **1421.** ► The Book of Ecclesiastes contains this famous passage concerning the idea of 'a time for all things'...?

HISTORY   **1422.** ► How many years did the Ottoman Empire rule over the land of Israel (to the nearest hundred)?

LANGUAGE   **1423.** ► The Yiddish word *shtick* refers to...?

GEOGRAPHY   **1424.** ► The geography of northern pre-State Israel was mostly made up of this type of land...?

ANSWERS

CURRENT
EVENTS 1417. ► Israel is the only nation of the 184 countries included that has no capital city listed. Jerusalem is described as Israel's "seat of government." (Britannica officials claim that they received letters of protest so Israel's status was changed to end the controversy.)

WOMEN 1418. ► Gertrude Stein.

ARTS &
CULTURE 1419. ► Beta-Israel (literally House of Israel).

PEOPLE 1420. ► Eight (Ben-Gurion, Sharett, Eshkol, Meir, Rabin, Peres, Begin, Shamir).

RELIGION 1421. ► "To every thing there is a season, and a time to every purpose under heaven."

HISTORY 1422. ► 400 years.

LANGUAGE 1423. ► Literally it means "a piece" but most commonly it connotes a "theatrical routine."

GEOGRAPHY 1424. ► Swampland. (The settlers drained and filled in the swamps.)

CURRENT
EVENTS

1425. ► This Vice-Presidential candidate said: "The Palestine question is the cause of most international terrorism." This statement was later revised to: "Terrorism is not only or even predominantly a Palestinian phenomenon" . . . ?

WOMEN

1426. ► This Biblical heroine saved the Jews from the Assyrians . . . ?

ARTS &
CULTURE

1427. ► This Wisconsin born Jewish writer became director of the Israeli Government's Press Office, under Menachem Begin, and wrote Double Vision: *How the Press Distorts America's View of the Middle East"* . . . ?

PEOPLE

1428. ► This Jewish family provided Britain with the financing to buy the Suez Canal . . . ?

RELIGION

1429. ► The largest Hassidic movement in the world is led by Menachem Mendel Schneerson and is called . . . ?

HISTORY

1430. ► What was the name of the underground newspaper published by the pre-state Jewish revolutionary group, the Irgun?

LANGUAGE

1431. ► The derogatory Yiddish term *Chazzer* refers to one who . . . ?

GEOGRAPHY

1432. ► Moshe Dayan lost his eye in a battle in this country . . . ?

(Answers next page.)

ANSWERS

CURRENT EVENTS   **1433.** ► Hans Sedlmeier was a German factory manager who was recently exposed for being the confidant of this notorious anti-Semite . . . ?

WOMEN   **1434.** ► According to legend, God created this woman long before Eve as Adam's equal partner, but she thwarted Adam's efforts to make her subservient to him and was banished from the Garden of Eden. Eve was created to take her place . . . ?

ARTS & CULTURE   **1435.** ► This Jewish movie director was married to the late film star Sharon Tate . . . ?

PEOPLE   **1436.** ► This statesman said, "I am a Jew first and an Israeli second, for in my conviction the State of Israel was created for and on behalf of the whole Jewish people" . . . ?

RELIGION   **1437.** ► This animal was sent by Noah to check on the level of the flood waters . . . ?

HISTORY   **1438.** ► When and for how long did the Warsaw Ghetto uprising occur?

LANGUAGE   **1439.** ► Maimonides wrote his philosophical works in this language . . . ?

GEOGRAPHY   **1440.** ► When the Romans conquered Jerusalem, they renamed the Holy City . . . ?

QUESTIONS

ANSWERS

CURRENT
EVENTS

CURRENT
EVENTS   **1433.** ► **Josef Mengele. (He supported Mengele during his years of hiding and was the secret contact to his family.)**

WOMEN   **1434.** ► **Lilith.**

ARTS &
CULTURE   **1435.** ► **Roman Polanski.**

PEOPLE   **1436.** ► **David Ben-Gurion.**

RELIGION   **1437.** ► **The crow.**

HISTORY   **1438.** ► **In 1943, for 28 days.**

LANGUAGE   **1439.** ► **Arabic.**

GEOGRAPHY   **1440.** ► **Aelia Capitolina.**

CURRENT
EVENTS   **1441.** ► The U.S. sent AWAC planes to this
            Mideast nation in an attempt to pre-
            vent Libyan aerial attacks on this other
            Mideast nation . . . ?

WOMEN   **1442.** ► This world renowned Jewish sculptress
            changed her name from Louise Berli-
            awsky to . . . ?

ARTS &
CULTURE   **1443.** ► This famous old-time Jewish comedian
            was one of the first men to dress in drag
            during his act . . . ?

PEOPLE   **1444.** ► His philosophical treatise, *The Star of
            Redemption*, has had a profound effect
            on Jewish as well as Christian
            theologians . . . ?

RELIGION   **1445.** ► The religious books of the Jews teach
            that the world is based upon three
            things: on justice, on truth, and on . . . ?

HISTORY   **1446.** ► Judah the Maccabee conquered
            Jerusalem in this year . . . ?

LANGUAGE   **1447.** ► The pejorative Yiddish term *shlepper*
            refers to . . . ?

GEOGRAPHY   **1448.** ► This Mideast nation is known as the
            Hashemite Kingdom . . . ?

ANSWERS

1441. ► Egypt was preparing to help defend Sudan against a feared Libyan invasion.

WOMEN **1442.** ► Louise Nevelson.

ARTS & CULTURE **1443.** ► Milton Berle.

PEOPLE **1444.** ► Franz Rosenzweig.

RELIGION **1445.** ► Peace.

HISTORY **1446.** ► 165 B.C.E.

LANGUAGE **1447.** ► One who is an embarrassment or a stupid oaf.

GEOGRAPHY **1448.** ► Jordan.

CURRENT
EVENTS   1449. ► The recent Vatican statement on the "Chosenness" of the Jewish people dismayed the world Jewish community because...?

WOMEN   1450. ► Founded in 1893, by Hannah G. Solomon, the original purpose of this women's organization was to further the cause of religious education and philanthropy...?

ARTS &
CULTURE   1451. ► This French author wrote the dreadful book *The Inequality of Human Races.* His ideas concerning the purity of certain races were later adopted by the Germans to forge the concept of Aryan superiority...?

PEOPLE   1452. ► This Jewish scientist was the "father of computing"...?

RELIGION   1453. ► This noted rabbi discovered the *Genizah* in Cairo...?

HISTORY   1454. ► In the early 1960's, David Ben-Gurion, Shimon Peres and Moshe Dayan broke from the Labor party to form...?

LANGUAGE   1455. ► Tel Aviv's *Adloyade* parade is known in English as...?

GEOGRAPHY   1456. ► Muhammed, the founder of Islam, exiled or killed the Jews of Arabia who did not convert in this city...?

ANSWERS

1449. ► They suggested the Jews were "chosen" to prepare for the coming of Christ.

1450. ► The National Council of Jewish Women.

1451. ► Count Gobineau.

1452. ► John von Neuman.

1453. ► Solomon Schechter.

1454. ► Rafi.

1455. ► Purim Parade.

1456. ► Jerusalem.

CURRENT
EVENTS   **1457.** ► If the Peres-Shamir coalition government stays intact, when will the next Israeli elections take place?

WOMEN   **1458.** ► *Shelo Assani Ishah* is the traditional (chauvinist) blessing that an observant man recites every morning thanking God for not having done this to him . . . ?

ARTS &
CULTURE   **1459.** ► This heralded Jewish scientist served Israel's Hebrew University as head of its Academic Council. . . ?

PEOPLE   **1460.** ► This gentile author wrote a bestselling Holocaust book which exposed the failure of the civilized world to do very much to respond to the destruction of European Jewry during World War II . . . ?

RELIGION   **1461.** ► What restrictions are placed on gentiles participating in the Passover Seder?

HISTORY   **1462.** ► He was the only Jew to serve as Prime Minister of Italy. . . ?

LANGUAGE   **1463.** ► *Amen*, the word stated after all prayers by Jews, is derived from a Hebrew word that in English means . . . ?

GEOGRAPHY   **1464.** ► Near the settlement of *Zikhron Ya'akov* is a memorial known as "*Ramat-Hamadir*" or the Benefactor's Height. What is this?

ANSWERS

1457. ► 1988.

1458. ► "Who has not created me a woman."

1459. ► Albert Einstein.

1460. ► David Wyman, "The Abandonment of the Jews."

1461. ► They may not participate in any of the religious parts of the Seder. (They may, however, read the Haggadah and celebrate the Jewish emancipation from slavery.)

1462. ► Luigi Lazzatti.

1463. ► Belief.

1464. ► It is the tomb of Baron Edmund de Rothschild (one of the great benefactors of Israel who helped found the town in 1882).

CURRENT
EVENTS **1465.** ► Which Israeli politician recently insulted the American Jewish Congress and The World Jewish Congress by saying their international missions trespassed on Israel's primacy as the exclusive negotiator of Israeli-Arab and international Jewish issues adding that the AJC was a "peanut-sized organization?"

WOMEN **1466.** ► Miriam's punishment for gossiping about Moses was?

ARTS &
CULTURE **1467.** ► In the 1940's, which Jewish freedom fighter wrote under the pen-name Ben Ze'ev?

PEOPLE **1468.** ► This American business giant printed the forged *Protocols of the Elders of Zion* in a newspaper he owned and regularly promoted stories about Jewish conspiracies to take over America . . . ?

RELIGION **1469.** ► This Palestinian rabbi said, "One should say little but do much" . . . ?

HISTORY **1470.** ► Uriah P. Levy, a Jewish captain in the United States Navy is noted in history for this humanitarian accomplishment . . . ?

LANGUAGE **1471.** ► Deuteronomy is a word derived from this language . . . ?

GEOGRAPHY **1472.** ► This Jerusalem Gate is named after a King of Israel . . . ?

ANSWERS

1465. ► Vice-Premier Shamir said this (in September 1985).

1466. ► To catch leprosy.

1467. ► Menachem Begin. (This was a combination of his own father's name and Ze'ev Jabotinsky's.)

1468 ► Henry Ford, in the 1920's.

1469. ► Shammai. (He was vice-president of the Sanhedrin.)

1470. ► He was responsible for the abolishment of corporal punishment in the U.S. Navy.

1471. ► Greek. (It means Second Law.)

1472. ► Herod's Gate.

CURRENT
EVENTS   **1473.** ► Some Reform rabbis and a few small Jewish organizations who support Israel's Peace Now movement are seeking to expand the controversial appearances by these people in U.S. synagogues...?

WOMEN   **1474.** ► Ultra-Orthodox men and women engage in this summertime recreation separately...?

ARTS &
CULTURE   **1475.** ► This classic Jewish film was based upon the idea of Jewish exorcisms...?

PEOPLE   **1476.** ► What 2 major government positions did Levi Eshkol hold simultaneously during Israel's early years?

RELIGION   **1477.** ► This sentence in Proverbs emphasizes the importance of domestic peace. It begins: "Better is a dry morsel, and quietness therewith"...?

HISTORY   **1478.** ► The term *Etzel* was an acronym for this pre-State of Israel Jewish defense organization...?

LANGUAGE   **1479.** ► What is the difference between *"shloch"* and *"shlock"*...?

GEOGRAPHY   **1480.** ► The most famous ancient Roman aquaducts in Palestine are located in ...?

(Answers next page.)

ANSWERS

1473. ► Palestinian Arabs. They have been speaking in a few U.S. synagogues in recent years hoping to get across to American Jews the Palestinian view on the Arab-Israeli conflict.

1474. ► Going to the beach and swimming. (This is done to preserve modesty.)

1475. ► "The Dybbuk."

1476. ► Defense Minister and Prime Minister.

1477. ► ". . . than a house full of feasting with strife."

1478. ► The Irgun Zvie Leumi, or National Military Organization, which was led by Menachem Begin. (It spearheaded the 1940's revolt that drove the British out of Palestine and paved the way for the creation of Israel.)

1479. ► The former is an untidy slob; the latter means shoddy merchandise or junk.

1480. ► Caesarea.

CURRENT
EVENTS

1481. ► What will be the significance to Israel when Spain joins the European Common Market in 1986?

WOMEN

1482. ► The most prominent female *Talmudic* scholar, she was from the city of Tiberias...?

ARTS &
CULTURE

1483. ► This old-time comedian used the names Willie Delight, Buddy Links, and Captain Betts during his days in vaudeville...?

PEOPLE

1484. ► After the turn of the century, Jewish architect Henry Goldmark designed one of the greatest feats of civil engineering that the world had ever seen. What was this famous water project?

RELIGION

1485. ► Six hundred thousand souls were privy to the most manifest mystical experience of Judaism—the Divine revelation which occurred here...?

HISTORY

1486. ► Israel's equivalent to the U.S. Federal Bureau of Investigation is...?

LANGUAGE

1487. ► The Yiddish term *Pisk* describes one who is...?

GEOGRAPHY

1488. ► Most of the Jews in the world live in these three countries...?

(Answers next page.)

ANSWERS

1481. ► Spain will finally have to fully recognize Israel. (The Common Market requires all its members to have relations with the Jewish State. This is more an economic and political decision rather than a change in Spain's diplomatic views.)

WOMEN **1482.** ► Bruria.

ARTS &
CULTURE **1483.** ► George Burns.

PEOPLE **1484.** ► The locks of the Panama Canal.

RELIGION **1485.** ► On Mount Sinai.

HISTORY **1486.** ► The Shin Bet (it oversees domestic intelligence and counterespionage operations).

LANGUAGE **1487.** ► A big mouth.

GEOGRAPHY **1488.** ► The United States, Israel and the Soviet Union.

CURRENT
EVENTS
1489. ▶ This one highly controversial political decision of President Reagan's upset the world Jewish community more than any other act of his Presidency...?

WOMEN
1490. ▶ This female Jewish scientist won a Nobel Prize for her medical research...?

ARTS &
CULTURE
1491. ▶ This famous book about Israel and Jerusalem, written by Dominique Lapierre and Larry Collins, recalled life in Israel in 1948...?

PEOPLE
1492. ▶ What was the name of the South African Jewish doctor who helped Ghandi in India?

RELIGION
1493. ▶ While the Jewish people were escaping from Egypt, a double portion of *Manna* fell from heaven for them to eat on the *Sabbath*. This extra food is commemorated today by the requirement that...?

HISTORY
1494. ▶ What was the purpose of Jewish patriot Francis Schrader's heroic 28-mile ride during the American Revolution?

LANGUAGE
1495. ▶ "Tehiya", as in Israel's Tehiya Party, means...?

GEOGRAPHY
1496. ▶ The Druze, generally live in this section of Israel and the Bedouins in this other section...?

ANSWERS

CURRENT EVENTS **1489.** ► The visit to the Bitburg cemetery to honor the fallen German soldiers and Nazi SS officers.

WOMEN **1490.** ► Rosalyn Yalow (in 1977).

ARTS & CULTURE **1491.** ► "O Jerusalem".

PEOPLE **1492.** ► Dr. Kalbach.

RELIGION **1493.** ► There be two loaves of Challah bread on the Sabbath table.

HISTORY **1494.** ► To warn the citizens of Charleston, South Carolina, that the British Fleet was approaching.

LANGUAGE **1495.** ► Renaissance or revival.

GEOGRAPHY **1496.** ► The Druze live in the North and the Bedouins in the South.

CURRENT
EVENTS   **1497.** ► He was the architect of the "Peace for Galilee" concept...?

WOMEN   **1498.** ► This famous Jewish Biblical figure won a beauty contest and then a kingdom...?

ARTS &
CULTURE   **1499.** ► This old-time Jewish performer has been called the "Father of Television" ...?

PEOPLE   **1500.** ► This 19-year-old Jewish immigrant came to America from Switzerland and started his business career by peddling shoelaces. He eventually established one of the world's greatest mining fortunes...?

RELIGION   **1501.** ► At the Passover Seder, what happens simultaneously with the mentioning of the 10 plagues?

HISTORY   **1502.** ► What does the Israeli *Mapai* party represent?

LANGUAGE   **1503.** ► The Hebrew word, *Herut*, as in *Herut* Party, means...?

GEOGRAPHY   **1504.** ► This sea borders southern Israel and Saudi Arabia...?

ANSWERS

1497. ► General Ariel Sharon.

1498. ► Queen Esther.

1499. ► Milton Berle.

1500. ► Meyer Guggenheim.

1501. ► A drop of wine is spilled as each plague is mentioned.

1502. ► The Israeli Labor Party. (Established in 1929, it was Israel's ruling party from 1949 until 1977.)

1503. ► Freedom.

1504. ► The Red Sea.

CURRENT
EVENTS
1505. ▶ The Entebbe hijacking occured on this American holiday in this year...?

WOMEN
1506. ▶ Published in 1895, it was the first independent American Jewish magazine edited by a woman for women. It boasted 29,000 subscribers at its height...?

ARTS &
CULTURE
1507. ▶ This Zionist author wrote *Old-New Land*...?

PEOPLE
1508. ▶ The memoirs of this Israeli statesman about pre-state Israel were called *The Revolt*...?

RELIGION
1509. ▶ The Biblical bread of affliction refers to...?

HISTORY
1510. ▶ In the early 1920's, many Jews became Bolsheviks, not for ideological reasons and not because they were forced to, but because...?

LANGUAGE
1511. ▶ The Hebrew word *Tanach* stands for ...?

GEOGRAPHY
1512. ▶ Approximately how many Jews live in Australia and New Zealand combined (within 10% accuracy)?

ANSWERS

CURRENT EVENTS 1505. ► On Independence Day in 1976.

WOMEN 1506. ► "American Jewess."

ARTS & CULTURE 1507. ► Theodor Herzl.

PEOPLE 1508. ► Menachem Begin (the sub-title is "Story of the Irgun").

RELIGION 1509. ► Matzah.

HISTORY 1510. ► The Bolsheviks saved them from the Cossacks.

LANGUAGE 1511. ► Torah, nevi'im, ketuvim. (It is the generally used Hebrew term for the Jewish Bible.)

GEOGRAPHY 1512. ► A total of 72,000. (There are 67,000 in Australia and 5,000 in New Zealand.)

CURRENT
EVENTS

1513. ► The present Israeli currency, the shekel, replaced the former currency known as...?

WOMEN

1514. ► She persuaded him to reveal to her that the secret of his strength was in his uncut locks. She then had his hair shaved and betrayed him to the Philistines...?

ARTS &
CULTURE

1515. ► In what movie sequel, starring George Burns, did Jewish psychologist Joyce Brothers play herself?

PEOPLE

1516. ► This James Michener novel is an historic comparative study of the old and the new Israel...?

RELIGION

1517. ► What is the *Keriah* ceremony?

HISTORY

1518. ► Lord Balfour once expressed his approval of Zionism to this famous and wealthy Jewish lord...?

LANGUAGE

1519. ► Visiting the sick is one of the most important commandments in Judaism. It is referred to in Hebrew as...?

GEOGRAPHY

1520. ► Name the two major sections of the land area in Israel known as the Galilee?

ANSWERS

CURRENT EVENTS
1513. ► The Lira.

WOMEN
1514. ► Delilah.

ARTS & CULTURE
1515. ► In "Oh God, Book II."

PEOPLE
1516. ► "The Source."

RELIGION
1517. ► The cutting of a garment to symbolize one's grief after a close relative passes away.

HISTORY
1518. ► Lord Rothschild.

LANGUAGE
1519. ► Bikur Cholim.

GEOGRAPHY
1520. ► The Upper and the Lower.

CURRENT
EVENTS   **1521.** ▶ Once a fighter against Israel, this Christian Lebanese patriot led the pro-Israeli Southern Lebanese Army until his death in 1984 . . . ?

WOMEN   **1522.** ▶ According to the _Midrash,_ a woman who abandons the laws of _niddah_ or separation between husband and wife during the wife's menstrual period will . . . ?

ARTS &
CULTURE   **1523.** ▶ The most utilized musical instrument in Yiddish life has been . . . ?

PEOPLE   **1524.** ▶ This book is known as Saul Bellow's "most Jewish book." It is about an American professor and his private thoughts . . . ?

RELIGION   **1525.** ▶ This musical instrument was introduced into Reform Jewish synagogue services . . . ?

HISTORY   **1526.** ▶ This Spanish Jew claimed descent from the royal house of David, was a financial advisor to Queen Isabella and King Ferdinand, and spurned every inducement to remain in Spain after 1492, choosing exile with his fellow Jews rather than apostasy . . . ?

LANGUAGE   **1527.** ▶ These broad-brimmed fur hats, favored by many Hasidim for the Sabbath and other special occasions, are called . . . ?

GEOGRAPHY   **1528.** ▶ People of this Biblical city were afflicted with blindness . . . ?

ANSWERS

CURRENT EVENTS	1521. ▶	Major Saad Haddad.
WOMEN	1522. ▶	Be punished by death during child-birth.
ARTS & CULTURE	1523. ▶	The fiddle.
PEOPLE	1524. ▶	"Herzog".
RELIGION	1525. ▶	The organ.
HISTORY	1526. ▶	Isaac Abravanel.
LANGUAGE	1527. ▶	Streimels.
GEOGRAPHY	1528. ▶	Sodom.

CURRENT
EVENTS

1529. ▶ Israeli-Arab Knesset member Abdul Wahab Darousha created controversy by attempting to enter Jordan to denounce terrorism at the Palestinian National Council headed by Yasir Arafat. Arafat approved his visit yet he could not go because . . . ?

WOMEN

1530. ▶ Maureen Stapleton played this Russian-Jewish anarchist in the movie *Reds* . . . ?

ARTS &
CULTURE

1531. ▶ He was the first Jewish artist that the Vatican ever commissioned . . . ?

PEOPLE

1532. ▶ This Danish-Jewish scientist won the 1972 Nobel Prize in Physics and was the grandfather of Olivia Newton John . . . ?

RELIGION

1533. ▶ The Day of Judgement refers to this day—known by a more popular name . . . ?

HISTORY

1534. ▶ This "autonomous Jewish Republic" bordering Manchuria was established by the Soviet Union in 1929 to remove Jews from European Russia while providing "a non-Zionist solution to the Jewish national question" . . . ?

LANGUAGE

1535. ▶ *Shalom* is a tricky Hebrew word with these three meanings . . . ?

GEOGRAPHY

1536. ▶ In the Seventh Century C.E., the Arabs built a huge mosque on this Jewish holy site in Jerusalem . . . ?

 (Answers next page.)

ANSWERS

CURRENT EVENTS   1529. ► King Hussein denied him an entry visa.

WOMEN   1530. ► Emma Golding.

ARTS & CULTURE   1531. ► Marc Chagall. (He made stained glass windows for a large Vatican hall.)

PEOPLE   1532. ► Niels Bohr. (Olivia, however, was not raised as a Jew.)

RELIGION   1533. ► Yom Kippur or The Day of Atonement.

HISTORY   1534. ► Birobidjan. (Its Jewish population sank below 15,000 in the 1960's due to emigration.)

LANGUAGE   1535. ► Hello, goodbye, and peace.

GEOGRAPHY   1536. ► The Temple Mount. (The Mosque is known as the Dome of the Rock.)

CURRENT EVENTS

1537. ► This Denver radio personality was recently murdered by right-wing anti-Semitic killers...?

WOMEN

1538. ► She is currently the most popular female sex-therapist in America, appearing regularly on her own TV and radio talk shows...?

ARTS & CULTURE

1539. ► The English name of author Achad Ha'am is...?

PEOPLE

1540. ► He was the Jewish male lead in the movie version of the book that won Philip Roth the 1960 National Book Award for Fiction...?

RELIGION

1541. ► By profession a physician in 12th-century Cairo, he is sometimes called "The Jewish Aristotle"...?

HISTORY

1542. ► The medieval interpretation of the expression "wandering Jew" refers to a cobbler who did what...?

LANGUAGE 1543. ► The Hebrew word for "light" is...?

GEOGRAPHY 1544. ► "Aza" is the Hebrew name for this strip of land in southern Israel...?

(Answers next page.)

ANSWERS

1537. ▶ **Alan Berg.**

1538. ▶ **Dr. Ruth Westheimer.**

1539. ▶ **Asher Ginzburg.**

1540. ▶ **Richard Benjamin (in "Goodbye, Columbus").**

1541. ▶ **Moses Maimonides (otherwise known as Rambam).**

1542. ▶ **He harassed Jesus and therefore was condemned to his fate of wandering forever without a home.**

1543. ▶ **"Ohr.".**

1544. ▶ **The Gaza Strip.**

CURRENT
EVENTS   1545. ► Polls indicate that the majority of Moroccan-born Jews and their Sabra offspring vote for this Israeli political party...?

WOMEN   1546. ► This Jewish entrepreneurial giant in the world of cosmetics has a wing in the Tel Aviv Museum of Art named after her...?

ARTS &
CULTURE   1547. ► This Jewish songwriter composed one of the most popular Christmas songs ever written...?

PEOPLE   1548. ► This Jewish-style music is a mixture of jazz, ragtime and vocals...?

RELIGION   1549. ► Cheese blintzes are eaten on this holiday...?

HISTORY   1550. ► This European leader convened a "Great Sanhedrin" and looked to Jewish sovereignty in Palestine as a way of extending his nation's power in the East...?

LANGUAGE   1551. ► The Sephardic term for rabbi is...?

GEOGRAPHY   1552. ► The three largest U.S. Jewish population centers are...?

ANSWERS

1545. ► The Herut-led Likud Party.

1546. ► Helena Rubenstein.

1547. ► Irving Berlin. (The song is "White Christmas.")

1548. ► "Klezmer" music.

1549. ► Chanukah.

1550. ► Napolean Bonaparte.

1551. ► "Chacham".

1552. ► New York City, Los Angeles and Philadelphia. (Chicago and Miami are rated fourth and fifth.)

CURRENT
EVENTS

1553. ► More than 900 Jewish children from this Mideast country have recently been sent to America by their parents, who fear for their children's lives because of political unrest . . . ?

WOMEN

1554. ► This Naomi Shemer song won the 1967 Jerusalem Prize and was the anthem of the Six-Day War . . . ?

ARTS &
CULTURE

1555. ► An American Jewish mayor recently wrote this bestselling book . . . ?

PEOPLE

1556. ► This Israeli author wrote *For the Love of Zion*, and is heralded as the first major novelist to write in Hebrew . . . ?

RELIGION

1557. ► What is the only day of the year besides *Simchat Torah*, when it is considered appropriate to drink in excess . . . ?

HISTORY

1558. ► In 1215, the fourth Lateran Council of Archbishops enacted this discriminatory law that Jews had to obey . . . ?

LANGUAGE

1559. ► The Hebrew word *Hasid* literally means . . . ?

GEOGRAPHY

1560. ► The *diaspora* is comprised of these Jewish communities . . . ?

(Answers next

ANSWERS

CURRENT
EVENTS 1553. ► Iran.

WOMEN 1554. ► "Jerusalem of Gold."

ARTS &
CULTURE 1555. ► "Mayor" by Mayor Ed Koch.

PEOPLE 1556. ► Abraham Mapu (Al Aha-Vat Tzion).

RELIGION 1557. ► "Purim."

RY 1558. ► Jews had to wear distinguishing clothing so that Christians would be able to easily identify them.

1559. ► Pious one.

60. ► Anywhere Jews live outside Israel.

page.)

CURRENT
EVENTS
1561. ► This male Jewish astronaut is an astro-physicist and carried four *mezuzahs* with him during his recent space shuttle mission...?

WOMEN
1562. ► In 1975, what did Barbara Ostfeld Horowitz become that made her a first within the Jewish religious establishment?

ARTS &
CULTURE
1563. ► The *Jewish Daily Forward* had a widely-read column of letters to the editor called...?

PEOPLE
1564. ► The famous Chagall stained glass windows in Jerusalem's Hadassah Hospital are representations of these scenes...?

RELIGION
1565. ► This movement within Judaism has always been centered on its leaders who were noted as much for charisma as for piety and scholarliness. They have traditionally passed on their leadership, from generation to generation, in dynastic fashion...?

HISTORY
1566. ► What was Joseph Trumpeldor's first distinction while serving in the Russian Army?

LANGUAGE
1567. ► Someone who is *tsedrayt* is...?

GEOGRAPHY
1568. ► According to Ancient Jewish writings this city was synonymous with the pig...?

       (Answers next page.)

ANSWERS

1561. ► Dr. Jeff Huffman.

1562. ► She became America's first woman cantor.

1563. ► "A Bintel Brief."

1564. ► The Twelve Tribes of Israel.

1565. ► Hasidism.

1566. ► He was the first Jewish officer in the Russian army.

1567. ► Confused.

1568. ► Rome. (The symbol of the Roman Tenth Legion which defiled the Temple and destroyed Jerusalem was fittingly the boar.)

CURRENT
EVENTS **1569.** ▶ This industry today is Israel's largest employer with some 60,000 workers (almost 20 percent of the labor force) engaged in 150 plants...?

WOMEN **1570.** ▶ This Jewish woman is a Progressive Party member of South Africa's parliament and a lifelong anti-apartheid activist...?

ARTS &
CULTURE **1571.** ▶ Approximately what percentage of American dentists are Jewish...?

PEOPLE **1572.** ▶ This Floridian was the first Jew elected to the US Senate and was a staunch supporter of the slave system...?

RELIGION **1573.** ▶ These three Jewish leaders—Solomon Schechter, Cyrus Adler and Louis Finkelstein—were presidents of this Jewish movement's seminary...?

HISTORY **1574.** ▶ He was the first Jewish settler in the New World, arriving in 1645 in New Amsterdam, at least a month ahead of the Brazilian Jewish settlers...?

LANGUAGE **1574.** ▶ The Yiddish expression *Kopvaitik* refers to...?

GEOGRAPHY **1576.** ▶ Leon Blum was a distinguished socialist politician in this country during the 1930s and 1940s...?

ANSWERS

CURRENT
EVENTS   **1569.** ► **The arms industry.**

WOMEN   **1570.** ► **Mrs. Helen Suzman.**

ARTS &
CULTURE   **1571.** ► **Nine percent.**

PEOPLE   **1572.** ► **Senator David Yulee.**

RELIGION   **1573.** ► **Conservative Judaism. The Jewish Theological Seminary.**

HISTORY   **1574.** ► **Jacob Barsimon.**

LANGUAGE   **1575.** ► **A headache.**

GEOGRAPHY   **1576.** ► **France.**

CURRENT
EVENTS   **1577.** ► How many seats are there in Israel's parliament, the *Knesset?*

WOMEN   **1578.** ► Women who read from the *Torah* in Conservative and Reform synagogues are called...?

ARTS &
CULTURE   **1579.** ► The first refrain from this well-known Jewish song translates into "As long as in a Jewish breast the son's stirring has not ceased"...?

PEOPLE   **1580.** ► This great Jewish philosopher was a leading authority on Hasidism and is most remembered for his analysis of religion, explaining that it is a dialogue between man and God...?

RELIGION   **1581.** ► The founder of modern Hasidism, Rabbi Israel ben Eliezer, born in 1698, is known in Hasidic circles as the *Besht*—an acronym for...?

HISTORY   **1582.** ► Between 1901 and 1959, there were 319 Nobel prize winners. Within 20 percent accuracy, how many recipients were Jewish...?

LANGUAGE   **1583.** ► The sidelocks that many Hasidic men wear are called...?

GEOGRAPHY   **1584.** ► What was significant in Jewish history about Pernambuco, Brazil, in 1654 ...?

      (Answers next page.)

ANSWERS

1577. ► 120.

1578. ► "Baalot Keriah."

1579. ► "Hatikvah" or The Hope.

1580. ► Martin Buber (1878-1965).

1581. ► Baal Shem Tov which means "Master of the Good Name."

1582. ► 40 (eight were half-Jewish).

1583. ► Peyes.

1584. ► The first Jewish group that arrived in North America departed from this city.

CURRENT EVENTS   **1585.** ► Israeli exports of these products reached a record one billion dollars, comprising 20 percent of its industrial exports and representing a 20-fold increase since the 1973 Yom Kippur War...?

WOMEN   **1586.** ► This Biblical figure is the symbol of distrust in women...?

ARTS & CULTURE   **1587.** ► Jews seem to receive more Nobel Prizes in these two categories than in any other...?

PEOPLE   **1588.** ► This Jewish founder of psychoanalysis considered all religions to be irrational creations of the human mind which should be treated as a form of neurosis ...?

RELIGION   **1589.** ► This book records the mystical conversations of the second-century Rabbi Shimon ben Yohai, the most illustrious teacher and leader of his generation...?

HISTORY   **1590.** ► Christopher Columbus had this Jewish interpreter on his ship...?

LANGUAGE   **1591.** ► What does the Hebrew word *mafdal* stand for?

GEOGRAPHY   **1592.** ► Where is the location of the mountain on which Noah's Ark finally came to rest and in what country is it...?

ANSWERS

1585. ► Exports of military arms.

1586. ► Jezebel. (She was the Phoenician wife of King Ahab.)

1587. ► Medicine and physics.

1588. ► Sigmund Freud.

1589. ► The Zohar. (Some scholars say the book was the creation of the thirteenth-century Spanish, Kabbalist Moses de Leon.)

1590. ► Luis de Torres. (He reportedly attempted to converse in Hebrew with the Indians he met in the New World thinking that they could have been from a lost tribe of Israel.)

1591. ► The National Religious Party. (This was formed in a 1948 coalition with the Mapai party.)

1592. ► Mount Ararat, a mountain in Turkey. (The remains of a boat—reputed to be the "Ark"—have been discovered there.)

CURRENT EVENTS
1593. ► This Israeli political party is led by an American-born rabbi who calls for the explusion of all Arabs from the land of Israel?

WOMEN
1594. ► 21-year-old Golda Meir is remembered in a well-known photograph where she portrays this role in a play describing Jewish history. . . ?

ARTS & CULTURE
1595. ► This recent non-fiction bestseller was also a nine-part television series, which required four years of filming and research in 19 countries on four continents. . . ?

PEOPLE
1596. ► Who was Charles Dicken's leading Jewish character. . . ?

RELIGION
1597. ► This festival celebrates the beginning of the religion of the ancient Hebrews?

HISTORY
1598. ► Polish Cossack hero, Bogdan Chmielnicki, instituted a terror campaign killing hundreds of thousands of Polish Jews in 1648. He and his followers spared a Jewish life only if the person agreed to. . . ?

LANGUAGE
1599. ► A *crypto-Jew* is one who. . . ?

GEOGRAPHY
1600. ► This was the last independent and free nation in the area of Palestine before the creation of the modern State of Israel. . . ?

CULTURE
1601. ► The affectionate term for a woman married to a rabbi is *rebbitzen*. What is the husband of a woman rabbi known as. . . ?

ANSWERS

CURRENT EVENTS   1593. ► The Kach Party, led by Rabbi Meir Kahane.

WOMEN   1594. ► The Statue of Liberty.

ARTS & CULTURE   1595. ► Heritage: Civilization and the Jews, by Abba Eban.

PEOPLE   1596. ► Fagin. (A despicable child abuser and thief.)

RELIGION   1597. ► "Shavuos" or the giving of the Ten Commandments.

HISTORY   1598. ► Be baptized.

LANGUAGE   1599. ► Pretends he is not Jewish but secretly practices Judaism.

GEOGRAPHY   1600. ► Ancient Israel.

CULTURE   1601. ► Remit "responsa" on this question to: Ian Shapolsky c/o Steimatzky Publishing, 56 East 11 St. NY, NY, 10003. All mail will be answered.)

Look for Book III
Coming Soon

The Third Jewish Trivia and Information Book™
Trivia Judaica™ III

You can order the *Jewish Trivia Game*™ by using the forms on the last pages of this book.

STEIMATZKY
New York   Jerusalem   Tel Aviv

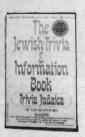